The Problem with our
Pursuit for Perfection

and the
Life-Changing Practice
of Good Enough

LYNNE CAZALY

ish

First published in 2018
Iteration 1 – October 2018
Iteration 2 – November 2018
Iteration 3 – December 2018
Iteration 4 – February 2019
Iteration 5 – May 2019

National Library of Australia Cataloguing-in-Publication entry:
Author: Lynne Cazaly, 1964 -
Title: ish: The problem with our pursuit for perfection and the life-changing practice of good enough
ISBN: 978-0-6482973-1-4

Subjects: Personal Development.
                 Leadership.
                 Productivity.
                 Change.
                 Creativity.
                 Self Development.
                 Communication.

Cover design, hand drawn font and layout by Lynne Cazaly.
gasp It's good enough.
Editors: Lu Sexton and Jessica Hoadley
Research assistance by Myra May Sabaldan Lahoylahoy

The Problem with our
Pursuit for Perfection

ish

and the
Life-Changing Practice
of Good Enough

ish

This page has been intentionally left
blank-ish

Dedication

To Noel, Shirley and Jeff

who showed me how to live a life

so very ish-ly

and to Michael

who accepts my ish-ness.

ish

This page is blank-ish too

Contents

Yep ... blank-ish.

About this book

This book was written using an iterative approach. That is, the first versions that were made publicly available in 2018 were rough and unfinished and seemed disorganised and imperfect.

But it was through these early prototypes that ideas and thinking about perfectionism and the idea of 'ish' were made available to people who wanted to read about it.

Readers provided feedback, comments and insights and I'm grateful to these early supporters who told me what they thought.

You're now holding the fourth, no, fifth iteration of the book.

Will there be more than this? Possibly: to tidy up some final changes, make corrections, pick up those elusive final spelling errors … and so on.

The point is, I could sit here and tell you one thing – which is to work in increments and to iterate your ideas and projects and activity – yet at the same time not walk my talk.

I could work endlessly on creating the best version of this book possible and only release it when it's 'finished', which may be never – because things can always be improved.

And that's what a perfectionist might do.

I'm a reformed perfectionist.

Instead, I've practised ish. I've worked in increments, received feedback and made updates. Accepting the principle of ish in my life has made me more productive, successful, and less stressed.

It's not perfect. It can never be. Nothing can. But it's available in all its ish-ness.

And now you hold it. Thank you!

Lynne.

Join the community

As you'll read, perfectionism can be a real pain!

Throughout this book I refer to resources, models and ways of thinking that can help you tackle perfectionism and adopt a more imperfect and definitely more enjoyable life. There are more resources to read about and download from
www.lynnecazaly.com.au/ishresources

Don't let a single read through of ish be the end of your learning; there are opportunities to join an online community where you can contribute your thoughts, experiences and shifts to the conversation.

Check out the online community, resources, programs and other stuff at www.theishbook.com/community

And if you're part of a Book Club, you can download discussion questions, ideas for reflection and other resources at www.lynnecazaly.com.au/ishresources

'To not do anything because it can't be exactly how you imagined in your head on the first run will hinder you immensely.'

Elizabeth Grace Saunders

INTRODUCTION

The first bit

ish

How often while you're working on a task or project have you thought 'It's not good enough' or 'I couldn't share that; it's not finished yet'?

We often have this belief that 'it's not ready … yet'. Yet.

Whatever it is we want to do with it – share it, send it, ship it, sell it, show it … or sometimes, to simply tell someone about it – we think there's still work to be done to make it 'good enough'.

This is because we've been brought up with cultural, societal and social expectations that place great value on achievement, success and excellence. Striving for perfection is something we've been encouraged to do for most of our lives.

We hear sayings like:

- the meal was cooked to perfection
- the music was pitch perfect
- picture perfect

and of course:

- practice makes perfect.

There is an increasing attention – almost a fixation – on ridiculously and impossibly high standards. Advertising campaigns and society at large seem to send us messages about desiring perfection:

- a product or treatment that might give us a flawless complexion

- a creation or performance that is said to be 'faultless'

- the perfect solution to a troublesome problem

and sometimes the single-word answer out of our mouths is simply … 'Perfect!'

When we're in a learning environment – learning a new skill, trying something new - we often want to know if what we've done is right. Is it correct? Did we do it to the standard that was required? Are we fearful of messing things up, making a mistake or looking foolish and doing less than our 'best'?

Still other situations in our daily lives might cause us to think that things need to be exact, precise, correct, thorough, 100%, impeccable and spotless. This might be at home, in the car, the thing we're making, baking, creating or starting, the project we're working on, the job we have, the relationship we're in, the business we're thinking of starting, the family we're making, the event we're planning, the web site we're launching, the book we're writing. *gulp*

We also hear people being described in a perfect way as being fastidious or meticulous, diligent, thorough, hair-splitting, or a stickler for perfection.

I heard someone called a 'fusspot' recently because what they asked for had to be so precise and specific to their requirements. Aren't some rock and roll musicians known to be 'divas' when they ask for the brown M&Ms to be separated from the rest of the colours? And who was it that demanded each colour be put in a separate bowl?

Many a performer has refused to step on stage until their 'rider' – the drinks and requirements in their dressing room - were 'just so'. Whether it's a fear that this slight change to a routine or ritual will bring bad luck or they're just deeply into the habit of having everything perfect in their mind, there are some things we seek perfection on that are vital ... and others are downright silly.

What's with all this perfection? Do we really desire, notice, want, demand, expect and believe we require perfect? All the time? For everything?

I'm here to say no. It's usually unrealistic, unnecessary and counterproductive.

Sure, there are contexts when exactness is vital: I'm thinking of aeroplane design, surgery, bridge construction, food handling ... and a myriad of other industries and sectors.

But there are certainly many other times, every day, when 'good enough' is plenty good enough.

I'm a great advocate for the next few phrases:

- perfect is the enemy of good

- near enough is good enough
- that will do the job

and

- nobody's perfect.

And of course ... nobody *is* perfect. As the genius physicist, cosmologist and author Stephen Hawking explained, 'One of the basic rules of the universe is that nothing is perfect. Perfection simply doesn't exist. Without imperfection, neither you nor I would exist.'

So, why are we trying so hard? The thing is, many of us are busier than ever, with a to-do list that has no end.

There's always something else that can be done. We never seem to run out of things to do. Even the celebration of emptying an email inbox to zero is losing its thrill; it just fills up again the next day!

Getting things done in life matters, sure. But getting the important things – important to us – done, matters more.

And, if we spend a lot of time trying to make one thing perfect, how can we ever get anything done?

As a reformed perfectionist, I want to share what I've learned about living by the principle of 'ish' and how it can help you get on with living the great life that we're here for.

PART 1

THE WHAT & WHY BIT

ish

CHAPTER 1

The perfectionist transformed bit

ish

I've been running my own business for more than twenty years.

In the early days of deciding to go it alone and ditch the full-time job, then launching and marketing my business, I experienced many hurdles, hiccups and downright disasters courtesy of my endless pursuit of trying to make things better, no, perfect.

Like most people, I'd had my fair share of perfectionist bosses and their ethos, expectations and behaviour had rubbed off. I always felt that nothing I did was good enough for my business to share, show, publish or send out. Everything could be better if I just put in that little bit more effort, stayed that bit later, pulled an all-nighter, came in early, worked through the weekend or took work home … does this sound familiar?

I wish I could tell you that I had one 'aha' moment when I realised that I was wasting my time, looking for something that was unattainable. But it wasn't quite one aha moment, it was a pairing of two unlikely situations: software developers, and Theatresports improvisation.

The ish of improvisation

I loved watching *Whose Line Is It Anyway?* the improvisation comedy show originally hosted by Drew Carey, and also attending the season performance of *Theatresports* each year. *Theatresports* is a theatre game where teams compete against each other in improvised performances on stage. No script. No preparation. No rehearsal. They do some warm up exercises to get ready though.

Sometimes the scenes were prompted by a line of dialogue from the audience, sometimes by a sound effect, or a particular improv game. Sometimes scenes turned out funny, and sometimes emotional. Improvisers are seemingly very clever because they operate from a set of principles that help them work well together and generate great ideas, creating the performance you see before you on stage.

At the end of a performance by my local group, *Impro Melbourne,* they promoted their public workshops and I thought

'Why not?' I'd go along and learn.

Over the next year I enjoyed semesters of courses with topics and titles like 'Spontaneity', 'Character' and 'Narrative', filled with activities, exercises, creative games and skills sessions.

I remember wanting to be good at it. To be a perfect improviser. I didn't want to look foolish. I wanted to be clever, funny, quick and competent.

But as those early weeks went by, and as I learned more about how creativity works, how to use spontaneity to work together in an ensemble, and how to trust yourself, I realised I'd been letting 'perfect' most certainly be the enemy of good in my life.

Keith Johnstone, a guru of improvisation, wrote the book *Impro: Improvisation and the Theatre*. I found it to be incredibly insightful and applicable beyond the stage. It was full of practical ideas about life, learning and getting things done. I realised how much and how often we censor ourselves, doubt ourselves, hesitate and filter and wonder and worry. And all because we don't want to fail or don't want to look foolish.

As the months of improvisation training went by I relaxed into it, learning more, trusting myself more, failing more – and the sky didn't fall in. Fun ensued. The whole experience became better, easier, more enjoyable, and less stressful. The opportunity then came for us students of improvisation to perform with the Impro Melbourne team in the next season of *Theatresports*, on stage – not in the main performance, but in the first half, a bit like entrée.

'What if I mess up? What if I look silly?' Here was that voice of perfection trying to make me scared, trying to make me back out, or at least postpone until next year when I'd be better – more experienced. But I pressed pause on this thought pattern: what if I just do what I've learned, and see what happens? What if I approach it all like a kind of experiment?

How cool is improv; to put something out there that you've just made up! And if it's not perfect, it doesn't matter. In fact, that's what makes it so good. It's not perfect.

Ten weeks of entrée performances with Impro Melbourne's Theatresports season followed. There were certainly some funny scenes, some successful scenes, some huge laughs, a few tears and a wonderful camaraderie from the team and group that performed throughout the season. It was all w-a-y good enough.

The ish of software development

Just a few months later, while I was delivering some consulting and training services to a financial services company, the project lead, Jay, took me on a tour of the technical team's area where they were designing and implementing the project. As Jay opened the door and walked into one of the rooms, he said 'This is where it's all happening!'

It was not unlike a war room on those political dramas like *House of Cards* or *The West Wing*: there were people sitting around a main table, TV monitors lining the walls with information flicking across them, people working at computers, people getting up from their seats and walking over to a wall of Post-it notes and index cards and moving those pieces of paper along the wall. I was witnessing my first experience of agile software developers, busily coding and work on the developing software that would business's back-end technology and run the applications that financial advisers would use.

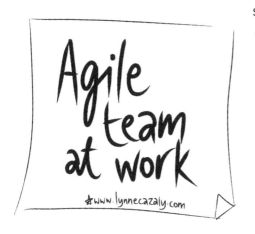

'Ding!' Someone tapped on a bell like you see at unattended reception desks.

'That means they've just launched some software,' said Jay.

'Really? Already?' I asked.

'Yep.'

And before long, 'Ding!' another something launched and went live.

Here was this team, pushing work out the door – well, out through the internet – and it was live for clients to use. Right then and there. 'But what if something's wrong with it?' I asked. 'They'll pause it, improve on it and then push it out there again,' Jay said. 'Plus we get great feedback from the people who are using it right now. We know which bits work well and which bits might need a little more attention.'

Boom! My two worlds collided.

The performance, trust and activity of improvisation seemed to mix and morph with the performance, trust and activity of software developers; both of these fields are committed to getting things done while working from a set of principles, and both know that aiming for perfection most certainly gets in the way of getting things done.

Boom and ka-boom! I fell in love with the rapid progress the software developers were making, despite some of their first attempts not being perfect.

Since then I've done my best to embrace this ethos, attitude and way of thinking in my work. It hasn't always been easy, because the desire to pursue perfection often feels like a default, automatic and perhaps hard-wired, behaviour (we'll look into that in Chapter 3), but the more success I got from trying less and putting things out there that were near enough, the more confident I became that I was onto something – something that could change my life (and maybe yours too).

I realised that, despite my past pursuit of perfectionism, I'd had some very ish moments that actually helped me on my way.

My first accidental ish

When I first decided to dive into the business world I obsessed over the right business name – Lynne Cazaly and Associates? Lynne Cazaly Consulting? Colourful Rainbow Consulting? Oh, who knew! I sure didn't. But then a quick conversation with some work colleagues nailed it. We were trying to come up with a combination of words that involved my name and after a few minutes, seriously, just a few minutes, we got to Cazaly Communications – CAZCOM. That was it. The name was a good fit. It was good enough to go.

So I registered the name. Next step: get a business card. I went to a print-it-yourself kind of kiosk at a shopping centre, put $8 into the machine, typed in some words like 'Marketing. PR. Media.' and then my name, phone and email address (website not necessary back then). I pressed print. Out came forty business cards, one by one. I was in business. OMG! I remember looking around the shopping centre, seeing people going about their own business buying fruit or trying on shoes, and thinking, 'Whoopee! They've got no idea that my business is about to go live!'

But when I looked at the cards, I also remember thinking, 'They're not very creative, they probably need to look better than this', and 'I'm sure other people have better looking cards than this. They're not really good enough for a business like mine.' But they were all I had, and I had to start somewhere, so I went with it. Over the next couple of weeks I handed out all those cards. Without realising it, I'd ished my way into business.

Perhaps you can remember a time when you accepted 'less than perfect' and the sky didn't fall in. Life carried on, almost as if no-one noticed. Maybe you had to 'wing it' on an important presentation because your prep time was eaten up taking a sick child to the doctor, and everyone thought it was great anyway. Or maybe you put in a last-minute job application, wishing you'd had more time, and you got the job anyway.

We often ish when we have to. So could we ish because we choose to?

My first deliberate ish

The first time I deliberately chose to ish was terrifying, but it paid off. I'd decided to run my own public training program. Instead of delivering someone else's intellectual property on time management or leadership, I thought 'Why not run my own thing?'

I'd learned the skills of visual thinking (using hand-drawn icons and images to add to written words) to help make communication, influence and engagement more effective. I figured I could create my own course and teach people a mix of the visuals as well as the communication skills I already knew about.

I set a date for the course, booked a meeting room in

the Melbourne CBD and made up an A4 flyer that included a registration form. I sent it out to a few people and put it on my website. To my surprise, a few days later, a couple of enrolments arrived in the mail. People sent me cheques and put money in my bank account and I thought …

'Oh shit, I'm gonna have to run this thing! People are going to show up!'

It was only a few days away – I really hadn't thought anyone would sign up – and I had little time available to prepare the program before the workshop. But I went with what I had. Sometimes we think we have to finish things to the absolute best of our abilities. But no, not this, not me, not now. I delivered that workshop to a group of six people and I felt like it was messy, chaotic and disorganised. I wanted it to be better researched, more thorough, and more beautifully presented.

But you know what, the sky did not fall in. Even better,

the participants LOVED it. I had deliberately ished and it didn't matter.

I ran the program again and again and each time I was able to tweak it and adjust it based on feedback. Over the next few years, that program continued to be refined. I was able to run it confidently and competently, knowing that people liked the pieces that were included.

Here I was, totally feeling like those software developers, putting the first version out there and if it wasn't great, then pausing, rectifying and improving it, and then putting it out there again.

There was absolutely some improvisation in there too: trusting myself, making the most of my skills, listening carefully to the participants and not letting any muck-ups or mistakes get the better of me.

I still offer this program today and I've delivered it to over 10,000 people from different industries, countries, sectors, roles, teams, organisations and interests.

I've presented on it at conferences, run masterclasses, spoken internationally and even written a book about the skills contained in that first workshop. I've taken the thinking further and developed another keynote presentation … and written another book on it. It's continued to grow, grow and grow.

If I had let perfectionism talk me out of running that very first workshop for those six people, none of this would have occurred.

In the words of brilliant storytelling, Australian musician Paul Kelly, 'From little things, big things grow.'

'from little things BIG things grow'

Ish – How a suffix became a word

Ish initially belonged at the end of words like Danish, English, Swedish – and it still does – but over the years ish has found its own meaning, and that is 'approximately', 'somewhat' or 'kind of'.

Gretchen McCulloch in the article 'Ish: How a suffix became a word' cites some uses of ish in the late 1800s. Flip forward to present day and we apply ish as an economical response to questions like 'Are you hungry?' … 'Yeah, I'm hungry … ish.'

Ish often passes as the bulk of the response. Are you hungry?' 'Yeah … ish.' It's this pause that gives ish a meaning of its own.

This act of keeping the suffix and getting rid of the rest of the word is an example of degrammaticalisation.

In 2003, ish appeared on Urban Dictionary.

McCulloch believes ish isn't universally acknowledged yet – she wrote that in 2014.

My spell checker continues to underline it in red. *Adds ish to dictionary.

McCulloch concludes:

'… even when a word is a decade or two old, it can be slow to take root in the reference books, some of which are notoriously reluctant to add what sounds like slang. But there's no doubt that what may have originated as a Britishism is now firmly fixed in American English too. To not include it in our dictionaries is to pretend that it's not a word. Which means that, with respect to ish at least, we're so early '80s. Ish.'

Transitioning from 'not good enough' to 'good enough'

Pursuing perfection and never reaching it (because it doesn't exist) can make us feel 'not good enough'. Discouraged. The longer we hang out in that 'not good enough' space, the worse it feels.

The principle of ish can help get us up off the bottom of this ladder and into some clean, fresh air, where we are pursuing progress, not perfection, and we feel happier for it. Here's how it can look...

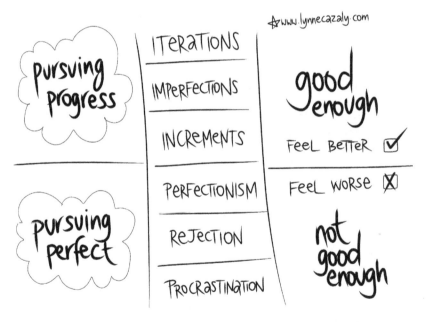

Actually, it needs to be bigger... let's give it its own page!

good enough — FEEL BETTER ☑

not good enough — FEEL WORSE ☒

Pursuing Progress	Pursuing Perfect
ITERATIONS	PERFECTIONISM
IMPERFECTIONS	REJECTION
INCREMENTS	PROCRASTINATION

The 'not good enough' space

Have you felt or experienced any of these three little nasties?

Procrastination – here's where we're stuck; we're just not getting started. This may be due to distractions, doubt of our ability, or fear of failure. We haven't hit 'go' to get moving on it. It's like sitting on a swing but not swinging or moving. The fear of looking foolish, mucking up or not doing a good enough job can all be behind procrastination.

Rejection – this is where we're judging, evaluating and assessing our own efforts and then denying or rejecting them thinking they're not good enough. We might diss them, thinking they're no good, bad even. We reject them first before anyone else gets the chance to.

Perfectionism – here we get working on a task or project but we think our progress still isn't good enough. We don't like what we've done. We criticize ourselves, yet continue to keep putting time into things trying to make them 'better'. We don't seem to know when to stop working on something. We might start a lot of things, but never finish them.

Down in this space it's a lose/lose situation. Things aren't getting done, and we're feeling bad about it.

The 'good enough' space

When we stop pursuing perfection and instead pursue progress, we'll start to realise that many things in our life are just fine when they're 'good enough'. This is healthier, as when we can accept something is done-ish, we feel a sense of gain, completion or achievement, rather than a negative feeling of failure, doubt, self-criticism, or incompleteness.

To get there, we can use:

Increments – that is, aiming to complete smaller packets or chunks of work, getting started, doing a bit, then doing a bit more.

Imperfections – this is when, despite making progress, yes, there may be a few hiccups, blips or blemishes on our early efforts or versions. But they're not crisis level blips. It's ok because next we find that…

Iterations – are a great way to test things out and see how they go. Here we're able to improve on things over time, putting our early versions 'out there' in the world and make them better over time … I'll go through all of these stages in more detail later.

But can you see how it's more of a win/win situation, not lose/lose? Things are getting done, and we're feeling much better about it.

Goodbye to that stuck feeling! Hello to progress!

The power of ish

Letting go of perfectionism and embracing ish – that is, moving up out of the 'not good enough' space and into the 'good enough' space – has changed the way I approach my business, which in turn has changed the way I live my life. Of course, I want to do the best I can, but I don't sacrifice my personal life to achieve that.

I no longer waste precious time chasing an illusion … because that's what perfection is: an illusion. And that's what we are going to look at in Chapter 2.

CHAPTER 2

The problem with perfect bit

'Perfect?

How can you define a word
without concrete meaning?'

Ellen Hopkins

What is 'perfect' anyway?

If you've ever pursued perfection, you probably had some sense, idea, image or hope in your mind about what you were aiming for.

Is it about being thorough or mistake-free? No blips or typos? Or is it about something looking and working just like you imagined it would? Is it about keeping pace with others? Or is it about receiving praise and applause because it was so good?

Whose idea of perfect are we going for? According to what standards and criteria?

Perfect is subjective. It's something we concoct and conjure up in our mind. We set an invisible and intangible standard for ourselves or others. It's an imaginary end point. In short …

… perfection doesn't exist, so it's impossible to reach.

Sometimes it is other people's standards that put the perfection filter over what we're doing. We don't know what they're expecting but we try to please them nonetheless. It might be a comment made in passing, or a vague description that's repeated several times; whatever it is, we believe it's communicating a standard and expectation requiring a particular level of effort, excellence ... perfection.

I heard a board member at a meeting recently say to their fellow directors regarding a pitch for a massive piece of business: 'Whatever we propose or submit, it has to be good. Really good.'

'Oh yes!' Everyone agreed it had to be good. Really good.

What is really good anyway? And when would we know we were there? When would the director be satisfied with the pitch? How would the pitch need to look or sound and what would the elements, dollars and details of it need to be? Who knew? It just had to be ... really good. The director also added vocal emphasis to it, stretching out the words: It has to be 'reeeaaalllllly goooooooood'. It was a voice of direction. His words were laced with invisible standards and expectations that none of the board or staff could see nor would they be able to work to... or achieve.

It's a never-ending quest

Because perfection doesn't exist, the search for perfection is a never-ending quest. It's a bit like trying to reach the end of the rainbow or the mirage in the desert. Just as you think you're getting there, it moves.

And this quest for the 'best', the 'better than last year', the 'better than ever'-ness will never deliver the satisfied feelings that we're hoping for. Marla Tabaka in her article '8 signs you're a perfectionist (and why it's toxic to your mental health)' says despite our search for perfection, we never feel perfect. Sheesh!

I see that the pursuit of perfection creates a cycle of disappointment and dissatisfaction. It goes like this:

1. PURSUE – I'm striving for perfection

2. REALITY – but I can never get there (because it doesn't exist)

3. PERCEIVE – so I feel crap about myself

4. BERATE – so I must do better, try harder.

Then we repeat, and create misery.

It could look like this, a prison or a trap that you just keep cycling through and around:

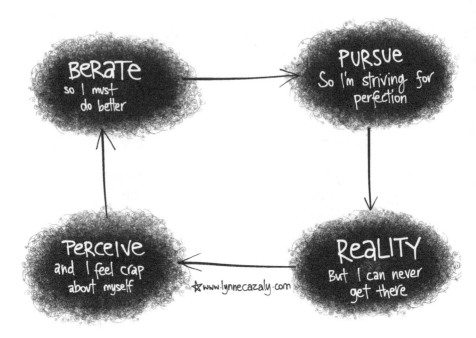

I'm not alone in this view of perfectionism. There's reams of writing and research out there questioning its value.

"Perfection is an impossible goal. Those who become preoccupied with it inevitably set themselves up for failure and psychological turmoil."

– Thomas Curran and Andrew Hill

Thomas Curran and Andrew Hill's PhD research about perfectionism is both extensive and captivating. Curran's TED talk, *Our dangerous obsession with perfectionism is getting worse*, is mighty insightful, too.

Curran and Hill define perfectionism as **'an irrational desire to achieve along with being overly critical of oneself and others.'**

This is one of the quotes I put up there on the slide show at my keynotes and conference presentations. And we look at it and read it and revisit it.

Irrational desire to achieve.

Overly critical.

Of oneself and others.

So Curran and Hill studied the differences in generations and perfectionism, taking data from over 41,000-ish (see what I did there?) American, Canadian and British college students. Using a tool created by perfectionism psychologists Paul Hewitt and Gordon Flett, the 'Multidimensional Perfectionism Scale' (see more on that in the pull-out box), data revealed that perfectionism is on the increase.

Along with their assertion that perfection is an impossible goal, Curran and Hill associate it with obsession, rumination, brooding, anxiety, shame, guilt, inadequacies and unworthiness.

Oh yuk! That all sounds like stuff we'd be wanting to avoid, not doing things to make it worse.

The researchers go on and thankfully suggest that there are much more healthier goals to chase after than perfectionism.

I'm with them on that one. Are you?

The types of perfectionism

Perfectionism doesn't just come in a single flavour.

There's a scale of perfectionism created by Paul Hewitt and Gordon Flett called the 'Multidimensional Perfectionism Scale'.

Two other researchers, Thomas Curran and Andrew Hill, used this tool in a survey designed to measure three varieties, or 'flavours', of perfectionism.

These are:

- **Self-oriented** perfectionism: holding yourself to impossibly high standards

- **Socially-prescribed** perfectionism: perceiving that others have unreasonable expectations for you

- **Other-oriented** perfectionism: where you place excessively high standards on others.

Curran and Hill had people agree with different types of statements like, 'When I am working on something I cannot relax until it is perfect,' or 'The better I do, the better I am expected to.'

The research was conducted between 1989 and 2016 and the results showed that perfectionism increased over those years, in all three flavours.

The second type, socially-prescribed perfectionism (where you think others are placing pressure on you or you can't fail in their presence) went up the most, by 33%.

Young people in particular are finding their 'social context is increasingly demanding, that others judge them more harshly, and that they are increasingly inclined to display perfection as a means of securing approval.'

The third one, other-orientated perfectionism rose 16% and the first one in the list, self-oriented perfectionism rose 10%.

Curran and Hill say the cultures they researched – British, American, and Canadian – have 'become more individualistic, materialistic and socially antagonistic'.

They say we're operating in 'a more competitive environment [with] more unrealistic expectations and with more anxious and controlling parents than generations before.'

'Perfectionism is actually a form of self-sabotage.

Other than nature's own design, nothing in life is perfect.

Perfectionism is a delay tactic that we use subconsciously to avoid being rejected.'

Vash Naidoo

It makes us hard to work with

Sarah Landrum in her article 'How being a perfectionist really is your biggest weakness' suggests that aiming for perfection can make us hard to work with. If we present as if 'nothing is ever good enough', it's tough to play 'team' with us.

As well as being tough to work with, perfectionists don't tend to 'go for it', says Landrum. They don't take as many risks because they're afraid to fail, so they stick with what they know. And they can't even celebrate their wins, because they're never able to live up to the expectations that they have set themselves.

Wow! I wonder if Sarah Landrum ever worked for my first boss, because she's summed her up to a tee.

My first boss was a perfectionist. I didn't realise it at first; I thought the problem was with me. After I'd been working there for a few weeks she called an impromptu meeting with me, closed the door and presented me with a typed list of my strengths and weaknesses. As if that wasn't enough, she then handed me a list of all the things she'd asked me to do that I hadn't done to her standards. This was my first job, for heaven's sake! And, sadly, it was my first exposure to the creature I now know as the 'perfectionist boss'.

I didn't realise it at the time but she was impossible to please. I was forever staying back late, working on the weekends, and putting in extra time.

Yet it was never, ever good enough for her.

There was always something wrong,

unfinished, undone or incorrect.

When we got to the end of a team project that had taken months of work, we never celebrated. The perfectionist boss always had comments about what didn't work, and what wasn't good enough.

Look, I'm all for continuous improvement. That's a different thing. But this was poisonous, ego-hungry perfectionism from someone who wasn't feeling too good about their own skills, role or capabilities. As a result, it flowed on to the whole team. We almost felt beaten before we'd even started the next project. Talk about low morale.

There is no doubt that working with a perfectionist is tricky. I had a conversation with a woman at an event (who'd read an earlier version of this book – when it was in its second or third iteration.) As we spoke about perfectionism, she was quick to let me know that her present boss is a perfectionist and it makes her working life hell. Her story is now some thirty years after my perfectionist boss story. This stuff is still very current, happening all over the world, in different fields, industries and sectors. A couple of others at the event also added that they too had worked with, no for, a perfectionist boss. It's interesting to note that correction they made. They didn't see themselves working 'with' the boss but rather as a servant, minion or lackey, working 'for' them, responding to their requests, changes, standards and expectations. It's as if the initiative, creativity and sense of adventure gets deleted from us and the work over time when you're working for a perfectionist.

It wastes time and effort

Years later, at the height of my own Perfectionist Period, I pulled an all-nighter on day two of a training conference in Barcelona (yes, beautiful Barcelona where the tapas and flamenco bars were calling me!) to refine a training program presentation for the next day. Why? Because I was stuck in the depths of perfectionism. My three colleagues and I had done plenty of work developing our program during the allotted time in the workshop, but we decided it just wasn't good enough. That we could do better.

So there we were (and there's a photo to prove it – see it on the ish resources page at www.lynnecazaly.com.au/ishresources) working all freaking night. I regret that now. It got to about 3.30 am and one by one we each had a lie down on an old couch in the foyer.

As if lying down for a one-eye-open nap on an uncomfortable couch with all this imperfection raging through my mind was going to make any difference. All it did was mess up my hair! We worked for another 7 hours. And for what? We presented our work the next day … and nothing extraordinary happened. We weren't drowned in applause and praise for pulling an all-nighter. There were contributions from other groups that were 'worse' if you're into comparison, but no-one thought any less of them. You can learn as much from what doesn't work as what does.

In choosing to push towards perfection I gained nothing and missed out on nearly everything.

Not only did I miss out on a group dinner and exploring the nightlife of Barcelona, but I also spent the next four days of the conference feeling like crap from a lack of sleep on top of jet lag. Was it worth it? Nope. Not at all. In hindsight, we should have presented what we'd done, got feedback and made some adjustments – we were in a learning program, after all – and then carried on, enjoying the program, the social connections and beautiful Barcelona.

My Barcelona experience shows what a waste of time and effort pursuing perfection can be. But don't just take my word for it.

Jo Wilson and Matt Plummer in the Harvard Business Review article 'The lie that perfectionists tell themselves' report on the idea that people equate time spent on a task with the quality of the work. We often think that spending another 30 minutes – or three weeks – on something will make a difference.

It usually doesn't.

It only makes us feel more confident in the quality, it doesn't really affect the quality. According to Wilson and Plummer, spending more time actually hurts our performance and reduces the quality of our work. Our thinking, emotional intelligence and problem-solving skills all diminish the longer we spend stressing over minutia, especially if lack of breaks or lack of sleep is involved.

We can actually do more in less because the 'extra' we put in doesn't matter.

In my experience, when I've worked back late or put in excess time on something like a report or presentation, I've absolutely ended up making mistakes like working on the wrong version of the document or losing changes I've made, or mucking something else up. It's as if the gremlins come out in force and deliberately cause us havoc. Wilson and Plummer explain how our engagement levels, decision-making skills and attention to detail decline and then so does the quality of the work.

Sounds like we need to quit that work once we've done a first cut of it, because from thereon, it's all downhill.

Researchers Avgoustaki and Frankort agree. They collected data from 50,000 people from 36 countries between 2010 and 2015 for their research into the effect of 'work effort'. They found that the harder people worked, the more likely they reported stress, lower satisfaction and inferior outcomes. Again, once more for impact: the harder they worked, the more the stress, the lower the satisfaction, the lower the outcomes. Urgh!

Working too hard burns us out and doesn't result in the success – career or otherwise – that we might be craving. We simply can't do it all and, even when we try, the outcomes don't go our way.

There's also the incredible missed-opportunity cost. What's the cost of spending all this time pursuing something we can't reach? What are we missing out on elsewhere? What's your Barcelona?

We've now seen that increased work effort isn't linked to increased rewards – rather, it's the reverse. There's clearly room for us to ease off on our perfectionistic expectations, and we'll look at strategies for doing this in Part 2. But first, let's dig a little deeper to understand why most of us think perfection is the gold standard.

Oh, let's just have a little quote from Brene Brown first…

'Perfectionism is a self-destructive and addictive belief system that fuels this primary thought: *If I look perfect, and do everything perfectly, I can avoid or minimise the painful feelings of shame, judgment, and blame.'*

- Brené Brown

ish

CHAPTER 3

The why do we seek perfection bit

'Perfection does not exist; to
understand it is the triumph
of human intelligence; to
expect to possess it is the
most dangerous kind of
madness.'

Alfred de Musset

I'm certain we're not born perfectionists. What is it that influences us as we grow up to pursue perfection?

What are we afraid of?

In a recent conversation with my friend Deidre, she recounted numerous stories about her family expecting her to do well. In fact, not just her family, but her teachers and employers did too. They all had external standards of perfectionism that they wanted her to meet – she was not totally clear of the details of those standards, but simply knew she had to do well at school and work. It was expected. Or else.

Or else what?

It seems there are invisible standards we're striving for, but then there are also vague and often feared consequences if we don't reach the standards.

Some of the things we might fear are embarrassment, failure, shame, regret, rejection and disappointment. We'll do almost anything to avoid feeling these negative emotions.

What are we trying to fix?

In her article 'Why perfectionism damages your life and 4 ways to overcome it', life coach Kathy Caprino says perfectionism is a 'learned, adaptive behaviour in our childhood,' and the causes originate in all manner of unfortunately familiar situations.

- It may have been that we didn't get the love and acceptance from our parents that we craved unless we achieved particular grades in school.

- Perhaps we were criticised by authority figures or compared negatively to others when we didn't achieve a high enough standard. Most of us probably have a story or recollection about how a teacher, community figure or family member or friend of the family came down on us for not doing well at something.

- If we experienced childhood feelings of being alone, scared and out of control, our reaction could have been to over-function to gain control among the chaos.

  If we had parents who were unreliable or erratic in their care of us, we might have tried whatever we could to overcome their behaviour.

No matter what caused it, says Caprino, perfectionism is 'an addictive, driven behaviour that damages your life, keeping you from fully appreciating yourself, recognizing your own worth and value.'

Addictive huh? And keeping us from fully appreciating ourselves and the wonderful skills, talents, gifts and characteristics we have … the things that make us uniquely us

What are we hoping to prove?

Do any of these resonate with you?

- If it's perfect, it shows I am clever and capable.

- If it's perfect, it shows I care.

- If it's perfect, people won't see how much of a mess I am.

- If it's perfect, then people will think that's how I do everything and that I am a worthy and valuable friend.

- If it's perfect, then I'll be held in high regard and esteem and people will envy me rather than me envying them.

- If it's perfect, it will prove that I turned out OK and am not at all like that teacher said I'd be.

- If it's perfect, people will like me, love me, accept me, notice me.

- If it's perfect, then …< add in your own … >

I wonder how much of our activity towards perfection is trying to say 'see me', or 'notice me' or 'please realise I am a human and I am here'. 'I am significant.' 'I count for something.'   *sniff.

I also wonder if there is sometimes some martyrdom in this? A martyr displays their suffering because it brings them more attention and focus. It brings reward and it feels good to have people concerned, worrying, looking at us, seeing us and giving us attention – for any freakin' reason at all.

Is there a must, a drive, a push to be perfect?

'I HAVE to finish it. It HAS to be perfect.'

Thinking further about this …

Is there a **connection** to us? 'I won't be perfect until <u>it</u> is perfect.'

Is it an **extension** of us? This project, PhD, assignment, DIY job, renovation, make up application, tidiness, craft project, meal, party or event, dress, outfit or speech is <u>about</u> me, it's <u>part</u> of me, it's got me <u>in</u> it.

Is it a **reflection** of us? Is it all people are seeing of us at the moment? Is it all we will *let* them see of us at the moment?

Is it the fear of letting people down or not living up to their (or our) expectations? Or that we believe we should do this or that? Or that something else wouldn't be 'allowed' or tolerated or accepted?

What are these expectations anyway? Do we not want to

disappoint someone?

Why did we take so much stuff on anyway? What were we trying to prove or demonstrate or show people? What was the message we were trying to say? Was it 'I love you'? Or 'you're so precious and important to me'? Or 'gee I'd miss you if you were gone' or 'I'm scared you will go'?

If you dig a little deeper into why you're being a perfectionist about something, you might discover a deeper belief or tendency which has nothing to do with the project, task or activity at hand.

What are we trying to say?

Two friends, both parents, were chatting to each other about the efforts they were making in creating costumes for their daughters for a school event. They both lamented the hours and hours of work they'd put in, despite their less than creative capabilities.

One said, 'That's how I show her I love her; it's what my mum did for me.'

Oh, my heart. So much love.

Are you putting an excessive amount of time and energy into something for someone else?

Is this action trying to tell them something?

Rather than being a perfectionist about something, might it be easier and more impactful to tell them what you'd actually like to say?

Millions of readers of Gary Chapman's book *The Five Love Languages* were introduced to the different ways we express our love and appreciation to others.

The five 'love languages' in the book are:

1. words of affirmation
2. acts of service
3. receiving gifts
4. quality time
5. physical touch.

Number two, 'acts of service', refers to things such as cleaning, driving, cooking or organising for someone else, instead of saying 'I love you' in words. Maybe we try to do these services really well. Showing love through acts of service can be part of a perfectly healthy and functional relationship – but not if we take it too far and perfectionism takes over.

The same goes if we are appreciative of our job role or involvement in a team or organisation: we might want to do the very best we can, to the very highest of standards, to show that we're thankful and that we are a valuable, worthwhile, useful member of the team. Again, it's healthy and commendable … until it's not.

Beware the 'curse' of wanting better

Beyond the internal or external confirmation that we might be seeking for ourselves, there are also life experiences that can drive a desire for more, or better.

Psychologist and author Barry Schwartz explains that as our life circumstances improve, our expectations rise. We begin comparing our experiences to those around us who are doing better, or to our past experiences that were better. He suggests we begin to suffer what's known as 'the curse of discernment'. The lower quality items or experiences that used to be good enough for us … are no longer.

Have you noticed this? Like at a café or restaurant, in a job role or even a car you've been in? Once you've experienced higher or better or more, your expectations may lift to a new standard.

'The hedonic zero point keeps rising and expectations and aspirations rise with it,' says Schwartz.

This means we may be living better, but we don't feel better about how we're living or what we're doing.

Schwartz suggests we need to settle for something that's acceptable, even if we know there is possibly, likely, most certainly, something better out there.

'It can be hard, in our culture, to force yourself to settle for 'good enough'. But when it comes to happiness and satisfaction, 'good enough' isn't just good – it's perfect.'

Seth Godin, in one of his many brilliant posts concurs:

'#perfect

Nothing ever is. Nothing is flawless, optimized and suitable for everyone.

Instead, all we can hope for is, 'the best we could hope for, under the circumstances.'

But, because there are circumstances, whatever happens is exactly what the circumstances created. Whatever is happening now is what's going to happen now. There's no way to change it. Perhaps we can change tomorrow, or even the next moment, but this moment--it's exactly what it was supposed to be, precisely what the circumstances demanded ...'

Pressure from all sides

As if our own personal drivers for perfectionism aren't difficult enough to unpack and let go of, there are also social pressures.

The world is full of mixed messages. Whether it's our idols, teachers, parents, friends or frenemies, social media influencers, images or advertisements, we're inundated with messages to:

- Be perfect – but natural.
- Be successful – but balance your life and career.
- Be healthy – but not a freak about it.
- Be active – but not a 24-hour gym junkie.
- Be into your hobby – but not obsessed and annoying about it.
- Be successful at work – but not too good that you make the rest of us look bad.
- Be pretty – but not dumb.
- Be clever – but not too clever that you make other people feel stupid.
- Be wealthy – but not so wealthy that you splash your cash around and make other people feel less than worthwhile.
- Be responsible, considerate, appropriate, polite, friendly, caring, clever, productive, beautiful

inside and out, bold, courageous, innovative, creative, thoughtful.

And then make sure you broadcast your perfect balance in everything through your perfectly curated social media feed with images of your perfect kids, perfect pets, perfect partner, perfect house and cooking prowess …

AAARRRGH!

Enough with the perfect!

Enough with chasing our tails and burning ourselves out for something that doesn't exist. Time to have look at how to break this cycle and make more time for the things that matter.

That's what we are going to do in Part 2.

PART 2

THE
WHAT
& HOW
BIT

'Too many people spend too much time trying to perfect something before they actually do it. Instead of waiting for perfection, run with what you've got, and fix it as you go.'

Paul Arden

CHAPTER 4

The what is ish and how does it work bit

'Striving for excellence motivates
you; striving for perfection is
demoralizing.'

Harriet Braiker

Ish isn't about doing things half-arsed and not caring, or over-promising and under-delivering.

Ish is about knowing when to start and knowing when to stop. It's about knowing when it's time to put yourself, your work or your ideas out there – knowing when it's fit for purpose, good enough for now.

We ish in our daily lives all the time, otherwise we'd never get anything done (how many times have you heard yourself say 'That'll do?') The trick is to understand how to ish in your work, personal, family, business and creative life as well, when it's appropriate.

Great hope, great work, great waste

Many of our ideas, projects, plans and proposals start with optimism and hope. Great hope. When we get working on them, we're doing great work. But at some stage there's a tipping point. You've got a couple of choices: you can 'go live' with your project, declaring it is done as good as it is, or hold off indefinitely as you continue on a fruitless search for perfection – a destination that doesn't exist.

Keep your eyes open for the path of great hope, great work and great waste. It looks like this. See the sparkly reward for going live?

Let's look at this a little more deeply …

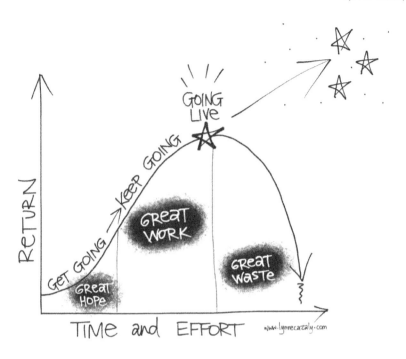

Great hope

At the start of a project or activity there's often a sense of great hope, expectation and optimism. We need that drive, inspiration and motivation to get us started and get into action. We're about to put in some time and effort! It's a little like looking forward to a holiday or an event or celebration. The looking forward is a big part of it, driving you towards doing what you need to do.

This stuff is known as a 'vision' for that reason. It's up ahead, we're about to embark on it, and it's exciting! It's important to 'get going' though, to get into action, to do things and garner some momentum. Otherwise, it's just hope … and hope is an expectation. It's got the potential to reek of procrastination.

Great work

During your task or project, you might reach a state of 'flow' where it starts to come easily. It could be hard work, but you're getting stuff done. You might say you 'broke the back' of whatever it was you were doing.

I see these stages when I'm facilitating workshops. The participants have great hope at the start of the day, then they move into a great work phase when they zip through the work that needs to be done.

But I also know that at some point, at some tipping point of effort, things will become tough. I call it the 'Groan Zone'. It's where you audibly groan. 'Urgh (moan) this is awful' or 'This is gonna be tough … urrrgghhh!'

There's a point right before overwork starts to become wasteful, though, and I call this the sweet spot for 'going live'. It's time to press the button, post the package, upload the page, show your work, send the thing, say the thing, do the thing, test the thing – otherwise, you're headed for…

Great waste

So yes, here we are. Not all of our activities, actions and efforts are of equal value. Not all of the hours you put into a project or task are equally effective.

When you reach a certain point of working on a task, your efforts aren't worth the results; the results aren't worth your efforts.

At this point the return on your effort from here on is limited. In economics, it's called the 'law of diminishing returns'. There will be a point where we don't achieve a reward equal to our effort. It's time to stop.

The waste of wasteful waste

If we keep trying to pursue perfection in a particular task, we waste a great deal of energy, time and effort, and create stress, worry and unnecessary overthinking. This includes overworking, pursuing multiple things at once, over-researching or endlessly gathering information.

What we need to do is look at the task and what we've done and say, 'You know what, that will be enough. That's satisfactory. That will suffice.'

These two words, 'satisfactory' and 'suffice', were cleverly explained by Nobel Prize–winning economist Herbert Simon in his theory of 'satisficing'. Yes, it's a thing. It's a decision-making theory where you look through alternatives and then go with the best. You make a choice. You make a decision. That will do. That is good enough.

Simon was also a political scientist and cognitive psychologist. He knew about how we make decisions and he gives us good advice saying 'decision makers can satisfice either by finding optimum solutions for a simplified world, or by finding satisfactory solutions for a more realistic world.'

Ish is about being a **satisficer.**

Satisficers:

- accept good enough,

- don't obsess over the options,

- move on after deciding, and

- end up being happier with outcomes.

The opposite to a satisficer is a perfectionist. Called **'maximisers'** by Simon, perfectionists:

- exhaustively seek the best options,

- compare everything against others to an unhealthy degree,

- expend excess time and energy, and

- end up unhappier with the outcomes.

While maximizing anything might sound like a good thing – think of super-sized meals and maximum returns on investments - the concept of actually *being* a maximiser isn't so good to strive for. I'm reminded of a friend who's still searching for the ideal, magical, perfect apartment. They're still looking. About six years later. Totally maximizing everything. Still searching for the best options, doing a-l-o-t of comparing (spreadsheets and tables and all the information about all the properties they've inspected over the years), spending countless weekends making inspections and talking with estate agents and still, still not happy with the outcome.

I absolutely get that making the purchase of a house or apartment is a big decision – but this is about living in one as a rental. A short-term rental. If they'd satisficed, they could have stayed in about 6 different properties by now and enjoyed all the fruits of living in all of those different locations. And learned along the way what they like and what they don't!

But won't people think it's not good enough ... I'm not good enough?

There can be a worry that if we ish a few more things in life – at home, at work – that maybe you'll be perceived poorly.

Actually, you won't.

As you'll see below, ishing won't change how you're perceived as much as you might fear for a number of reasons.

→ Spotlight effect

The 'spotlight effect' is the phenomenon of believing people are paying way more attention to us and what we're doing than they actually are. A counsellor explained to me that I was worrying too much about what others were thinking about me. The truth is, she said, 'They're all worrying about themselves – they don't have as much time as you think they do to worry about you! They're busy in their own heads.'

And this is the thing: we have ourselves as the centre of our world so we're often focusing on ourselves, thinking about what we're doing, looking, judging, wondering about what we're doing. All that detail about ourselves - and we think that others are noticing all that too in the same level of detail. But they're not.

When I'm working with leaders in organisations who are leading a change or transformation project, I warn them about assuming that everyone else is as deeply interested in it as they are. I'll say, 'No-one is ever as interested in your stuff as you are.' The spotlight effect makes it so.

This means you can ish more and plenty of people won't even notice. Will. Not. Notice. They're busy doing and focusing on their own stuff. Phew!

→ The paradox of imperfect

There is also a benefit to letting imperfections be imperfect.

The Japanese, in all their minimalist, orderly and technological glory, paradoxically know a thing or two about imperfection.

They were behind the lean manufacturing movement and the Toyota Production System, documented in *The Toyota Way*. They broke new ground, minimised waste and found efficiencies in making cars by deleting things that most of us previously thought were an important part of the process. How wrong were we? How efficient and lean were they!

And with an even more cultural advantage, Japanese ways of doing things have a beautiful imperfection about them. When it comes to ish, we can't go past the

Japanese concept of wabi sabi.

As Francesc Miralles and Hector Garcia say in their book *Ikigai: The Japanese Secret to a Long and Happy Life*, 'Japanese culture accepts the fleeting nature of the human being and everything we create. The key is to accept that there are certain things over which we have no control, like the passage of time and the ephemeral nature of the world around us.'

Wabi sabi inspires and teaches us to 'appreciate the beauty of imperfection as an opportunity for growth'.

Things change, they don't stay the same – people and ideas included. Rather than pursuing perfection, allow for imperfection, for flaws and authenticity, for the incompleteness.

The authors go on to say, 'This is why the Japanese place such value, for example, on an irregular or cracked teacup. Only things that are imperfect, incomplete, and ephemeral can truly be beautiful because only those things resemble the natural world.'

You may recognise kintsugi ('golden joinery') the ancient Japanese tradition of filling the cracks in broken things with valuable materials like silver, gold or platinum, not Araldite or super glue. This philosophy treats the breakage and repair of an object as part of its history: something that makes it more beautiful, not something to disguise. This idea shows us how we can look at ourselves, with all our cracks and flaws and bits that have been affected and repaired and cobbled back together. We're all beautifully flawed and wonderfully individual due to the paths we've travelled and the things we've experienced. Perfection is not required. We're already imperfectly wonderful.

www.lynnecazaly.com

There's great beauty and value in us all -- right now, just as we are. Good enough. Way good enough.

And anyway, it seems if we try to be perfect in an effort to impress people, our efforts may actually have the reverse effect. What? But how?

→ The Pratfall Effect

Cue the theory known as the 'Pratfall Effect'. This is a social psychology theory that says we find people more attractive – intellectually, humanly – after they've made a mistake. If we think they're highly competent when they stuff up, they're even more likable. (Funny though, if we already think they're less competent when they make a blunder, it doesn't endear them to us; we just think they're even less competent.)

The Pratfall Effect – where a 'pratfall' is falling on your butt or making an embarrassing mistake – is also known in advertising and marketing as the blemishing effect and it's used to great effect in ad campaigns and stories.

This is obvious in popular culture such as films and television programs. Characters become more likeable when we see their real and human flaws and failures; we see them as more like us, more likable, more real.

On popular nerdy sitcom *The Big Bang Theory* in the episode when Sheldon and Amy are getting married, Sheldon was having difficulty tying his bow tie. Yes, it's a tough and fiddly job! Amy said it was OK to mess things up, to not be able to do it. She quoted the Pratfall Effect to him, suggesting they'd be liked more if they appeared more authentic and human.

So, counter-intuitively, it seems that we can relax a little (actually, let's relax a lot), ease off the pressure and expectations about trying to be perfect because this whole pursuing perfection thing actually works in reverse. In reverse!

If we show our real, true, authentic and imperfect selves … we're perceived more positively. Crazy-ish but true.

While we might go for or demand the highest quality in things that really truly matter to us, we can accept a lesser quality if it does the job for us.

This leads us to acknowledge and appreciate the beauty of hand-crafted things. The imperfections in wood-carvings, the unique elements of our handwriting or the messy paint splatters on an artist's canvas.

Experiences of ish

Two advertisements for some tours in Melbourne, Australia, my hometown I saw the other day read:

- *The International Touring Sensation, The Dire Straits Experience, The Music of Dire Straits - Live on Stage.*

The second advertisement read:

- *Direct from sell-out tours in the UK and Europe, The Simon and Garfunkel Story.*

Do you see it? Or rather hear it? This is so ish.

It's not the *actual* musicians and bands of Dire Straits or the *actual* Simon and Garfunkel. It's a replica, it's somewhat like them. It won't be perfect because it's not them. And even it was them, it still wouldn't be perfect. It's somewhat them. It's partly them - their music. But it's not them.

It's ish. Dire Straits-ish. Simon and Garfunkel-ish.

Ish is everywhere around us, if we care to lift our eyes from our devices and pause on this obsession with and the pursuit for perfection. We will find that ish is in many places - and many, many people, thousands of people are more than happy with ish.

It's not actually Dire Straits. It's not actually Simon and

Garfunkel. But it's somewhat. It's their music onstage, theatrically presented.

It's like the Carole King musical, 'Beautiful'. It wasn't Carole but it was her music and an actor that sounded like her-ish. This happens all the time. We watch films with actors portraying greats like political leaders, sports stars and royalty. Meghan and Harry, I'm looking at you! We can't have the real version of the person because they're no longer with us or don't want to do the real thing or they can't act or don't want to tour or, it's 'not what *one* would do.'

Yet many people say that ish will be good enough and then it becomes an event and a touring extravaganza and people want it and they buy tickets! We accept it, enjoy it and it's good enough. Impersonators do it all the time! And we laugh when we hear them and we say, 'Oh they're good!!'

There is something in the arts, theatre, stage, musicals, performance, pantomime - where ish is enough for us. A few little costume elements will do. Our imagination will fill the gaps or we will say 'Yes that will do; I get it; you're trying to be this person or this animal or this thing in this location'. It's good enough, near enough for us to suspend reality for a moment and immerse in the experience. We allow and yield that the quality is not perfect, the performance isn't perfect but it is way good enough for us to enjoy and absorb, live and experience.

How many performances would you have walked out of if you were expecting perfect all the time?

If you went to an Elvis Presley tribute show and as soon as it started you screamed 'Pffft! That's not Elvis!!' stood up and stormed out demanding a refund?

You see we don't always need perfection. We like and love quality and excellence and greatness, sure, but we don't really need anything nearing perfection in every situation.

Back at the theatre, the efforts and effects created by costume, set design and production help to create an ish experience every single time. The music from the orchestra is ish. The performers are ish. They're very good aren't they, those Broadway or West End and professional performers. Even community and local theatre performers and school productions are so good too. They ish as well. It's not the actual person nor the actual soundtrack but it's ish and it's entertaining and it's good enough for us.

Did you hear about classical virtuoso violinist Joshua Bell who busked in a Washington DC metro station and no one really noticed who he was nor the quality they were walking past? He played for about 45 minutes, collected $32 in total from about twenty people and received no applause or recognition. This was despite being one of the best in the world, playing on an instrument worth about $3.5 million. He'd sold out a concert performance just a few days earlier.

Sometimes we can be near the highest quality and not even know it, and at other times we can think high quality is required or expected ... and it's just not.

And check out #nailedit for some glory about how imperfect is equal to winning!

There seems to be a common theme among those reality culinary or baking competitions on television and that is: amateur cooks or bakers should aspire for the standards in their dishes the same way professional chefs and bakers do. So often they're pitted against each other to see who 'wins'.

But Netflix turned this formula upside down by actually celebrating imperfection. Premiering in 2018, *Nailed it!* saw amateur bakers cooking up cakes and desserts and other sweet treats, trying to replicate a professional example. The contestant who most closely replicates the textbook example wins. But in contrast to all those other performance cooking shows, no one on *Nailed It!* ever does actually nail it. And that's the point!

Nailed It! has enjoyed its own meme and success on social media to affectionately and hilariously show how we didn't reach the standard or we didn't get to perfection like the photo in the cookbook. Whoever does? *Nailed It!* on TV has preserved the things about those cooking shows that work – which is often the person, their personality, their humanity, perhaps the Hero's Journey of the bake – and then it let's go and releases the pressure of perfection and expectation, allowing people to be imperfectly, deliciously wonderful. And we love it!

Australian comedian Celeste Barber's work on social media is another example of imperfection being a strength and it seems millions of people agree. She delivers imitations of famous celebrity snaps, you know, those beautiful yoga poses by the pool. But she's real and flawed and pokes fun at it all. She absolutely has #nailedit. And we love her all the more for it.

What to ish

Let's check out where and what we might consider ishing in order to improve our lives, get things done that are important to us and stop wasting time, energy and effort on procrastination and perfectionism.

I think you can ish in four ways as a starter:

1. Quality
2. Mindset
3. Activity
4. Time

Let's look a little closer.

QUALITY
what we make,
create or produce

MINDSET
what we think
about me, it, them

ish

ACTIVITY
what we do

TIME
how we spend
our time

★ www.lynnecazaly.com

Quality

This is about what we make, create, produce or deliver, in home or creative activities, in our own business or at work. We are likely setting internal standards for quality: 'It has to be like this', or 'It won't be finished until it's like that'. But the vision of perfection is a delusion. We don't get there.

We may do something well; it just might not match the expectation we had for it. And usually that is perfectly

OK. We can relax the expectation around the quality of what we are making or creating or producing or delivering.

As both famed management consultant, Peter Drucker and popular author and investor Tim Ferriss agree, 'doing something well does not make it important.'

Anytime at work when we're trying to make something better, to make it more acceptable is a sure sign we're on the hint for quality. When in fact we can often drop the quality and people often don't notice, or it doesn't matter.

A client of mine, Remy, was getting ready for a big workshop with the top-level leaders from his organisation.

Remy was going crazy over the quality of everything for that workshop. Everything! From the venue and the lighting, to the seating, the types of tables in the room, the colours of the Post-it notes, the types of coffee cups, the brand of coffee (OK, this is really important to some people, sure).

Everything had to be five-star, super-dooper and especially awesome. All of these hours of preparation and worrying and researching and running around finding the best of the best ... Remy was a mess! It's almost like he was catering to the needs of a bunch of fussy rock stars who wouldn't go on stage unless their needs had been met. The ridiculously high standards just weren't needed. It was overkill, and it was nearly killing Remy.

His high standards and expectations around everything for this workshop were impacting others who were involved on the day. They started to avoid Remy, rolling their eyes when he approached, knowing he was trying to find the 'next level' or higher standard on something.

I think we aspire for or go for high quality way too often. It's when we think:

- The design of the brochure isn't good enough, it needs to be better;

- The photo for the social media post isn't good enough, not creative enough; it needs to be higher quality;

- The meeting room space isn't good enough, it's not got the right kind of table or the light isn't right or the seats are mismatched;

- The gift for the team member who's leaving on Friday isn't good enough. Sure we need to acknowledge their great work and send them off in style, but are three people needed to go and research and shop and find the ideal, perfect, most wonderful-est gift of exactly the right quality and brand name?

There are definitely times when high quality matters, but you might find there are plenty of opportunities when ishing on quality is something to consider.

Mindset

This is our attitude or outlook about something – whether it's about ourselves or someone else, or about a project or task or experience.

We can be more ish in regard to the expectations we have about ourselves. We can be more ish in relation to others – we can relax our expectations of them. (Remember that one of the types or flavours of perfectionism is where we hold high standards for others and this is on the rise, causing problems for both parties.) And we can be more ish regarding the project we're working on.

At work, Jemma asked three colleagues to contribute content for a report she was working on. One by one, Jemma found that each of the contributors hadn't responded quickly enough, in enough detail, in the right way, in the right font, or with the right wording. Her whole mindset was calibrated towards perfection and these three contributors had no hope of reaching her standards. Throughout the collation of the report, Jemma was also beating herself up about why it was taking so long, was so hard, wasn't good enough or smart enough looking and would probably end in her losing her job. Her mindset was creating drama that just wasn't true, accurate or real. She could ish her mindset a little and reduce the pressure on herself and on others.

We can see and experience the perfection mindset when embarking on a new project. It's all the stuff we think about, the imaginary standards we set:

- It has to be like this

- It needs to look like this

- It has to work like this.

But in fact, we can relax our mindset and the standards we hold, the expectations we have and ish on some of this instead. It releases the pressure on us and on others. Phew!

Activity

Think about what activities you spend your time on. Obviously not the ones that are vital to do precisely (e.g. surgery, construction or engineering calculations), but everyday activities like our routines, housework, chores, general projects. These activities can be ished – they are allowed to be just good enough. They don't need to be the sort of thing you pursue perfect for. I'm looking over at the bench in my kitchen and there are 3 glasses, 4 plates, 2 water bottles and a dishcloth. All waiting to be washed and put away. I know some people who couldn't sit down and enjoy some Netflix or get to work on their brilliant business idea without doing the dishes first. But I wonder, is that the best use of your time right now? What would actually happen if you left the dishes there for an hour? Or until tomorrow? *gasp!

Wouldn't it be good if we knew when we're wasting time on an activity and when we aren't? The 'Pareto Principle' (also known as the '80/20 rule') can help us to find and eliminate wastes of time and energy.

Sometimes called the 'law of the vital few', it stems from Vilfredo Pareto, an economist who noticed that approximately 80% of the land in Italy was owned by 20% of the population. While it was in some of his earliest published works, it was management consultant (of course it was!) Joseph Juran who brought it to greater awareness, naming it the 'Pareto Principle'.

The principle suggests that 80% of our outputs or results come from just a mere 20% of our inputs or efforts.

The rest of what you do may not count for a whole heap.

This principle applies to customers, sales, wealth, finance, restaurants, airlines, shopping centres … even our wardrobes.

Time and again you'll find that 80% of the work or results, comes from just 20% of effort.

Many a relationship battle ensues over standards and expectations around the activities of the household. Visit or live in a share-house and you'll see how it plays out in the activities of the house. Yes, it can cause lots of disagreements and tensions – you might have to call a meeting to get it sorted – but it's a great example of how we have different sometimes invisible standards regarding the activities we do. For some people this matters less. For some, it matters more.

Picture this: at work, you go to the stationery cupboard looking for a pen. You open the doors and see the cupboard is in chaos. Thinking it would be helpful to other people in the team, or to simply make it look 'better', you start sorting, organising, tidying it up. In terms of activity, to ish would mean just working on it until it's good enough: a few minutes might make an incredible difference. Remember the Pareto Principle; 20% of your time will deliver a massive 80% of the effects or outcomes. A few minutes; huge results.

But the perfectionist might empty the whole cupboard onto the floor, get the cleaning products out, scrub the shelves, go to the shop around the corner and buy a labelling machine, go to another shop to buy organising baskets, label the baskets, sort all the items from small to large (and in alphabetical order!) and rearrange that stationery cupboard like a professional organiser. I know the neat freaks reading this might be thinking this sounds awesome. It's nice, yes, but is this amount of activity really the best use of your time? Is this level of detail your priority right now? It might feel good, getting control over something chaotic, but is this activity a shield or a distraction for the stuff you need to really be focusing on?

In this case, a quick tidy up of the cupboard that takes 7 minutes is likely better and more effective than a restructure, relabel and reconfiguration that takes 7 hours … unless you actually *are* a professional organiser.

With activity, we can often ish more often than we think we're 'allowed' to; like there are these expectations that we need to sweat over something and work diligently for it to be good; but we know and read about in Chapter 2 that effort doesn't equal reward. Anyone who's done a quick tidy up at home because some people are arriving in five minutes know this type of activity can be plenty good enough. In most Jane Austen novels – and the film adaptations – you'll see the household scurrying around hiding books, sewing projects, hats and wraps as a gentleman is downstairs, to come calling on one of the women he desires!

I was a house-sitter for a couple of years and I'd get to stay in some nice homes, looking after special needs pets (there was the three-legged dog, the diabetic cat, and the anxious parrot) whose owners had gone away on holidays. When the owners were expected back, I'd always do a quick five-minute whip around the house to just tidy, arrange, replace, dust, wipe and generally make it look untouched, or at least tidied. Yes, I'd done housework while they were away, but this was a quick, 'get it done, they're coming' kind of activity. Good enough!

Time

We can also be ish about how we allocate, spend, use, apply, manage, measure and keep track of time. Whenever we mean 'approximately' or 'near enough' about time we're being ish.

I heard someone on the bus the other day on their phone who said, 'I'll be there in 10 minutes. Ish'.

If you're allocating time in your schedule to work on a task or project, you might block out an hour, but think in your mind 'an hour-ish'. That means if you're done after 45 minutes, great, or if it takes an hour and 20 minutes, that's still OK. But if you allocate an hour and are still going on it 3 hours later, it's time to ish. You're in too deep.

Starting a meeting is another time-related thing. Some organisations are really strict. If it says 10am, it starts at 10am. No negotiation. Other times we can be a bit more relaxed until everyone arrives.

In workshops for example, I often say they start at 9.30am yet I'm OK if we start when the majority of people are there and that might be more like 9.37am. It can go too far though when you have a culture where people dawdle in to meetings when they feel like it; that's another issue and the standard needs to be reset in regards to time.

To recap: considering ish as a way to beat perfectionism, you can tackle things like

- Mindset
- Quality
- Activity

- Time

Sounds like lots of opportunities to ish, right? We now understand the value in imperfection, so can't we ish everything in life, all the time? In the next chapter we'll look at 'to ish or not to ish'.

ish

Chapter 5:

The 'To ish or not to ish' bit

ish

Ish isn't for everyone or everything, all the time.

Before you ish, check your task against the following criteria.

- Is ish doable?
- Is ish acceptable?
- Is ish feasible?

In short, does it matter if it's ish?

Sometimes 'near enough' isn't good enough. Like the builder's mantra, 'measure twice and cut once', we don't want to introduce any wastage or risk by being ish. Who wants to say 'near enough' to some building products, then you cut your wood and realise it isn't long enough for the job? Too late. Wood already cut!

Doable

When looking at a task or project, ask yourself 'Can it be done in an ish style?'

A client's workplace is contemplating setting up a gallery for their project: a central area with information and images about the project's progress where people are welcome to come over and look at it, talk about it, and work on it. Rather than everyone peering into their desktop screens and devices, they want to try and connect with other parts of the business and tell more of a story about the project.

Is it doable in an ish way? Certainly. It's not a project that they have to spend an extravagant amount of time and money on to get perfect.

In another example, a family in my community is planning to build a swimming pool in their garden. The architects are investigating whether it's doable on the existing slope, in that climate, with that soil, and within that budget, to meet regulations as required. Matters of gravity, science or nature might say 'yay' or 'nay' to the family's vision – but perhaps there is another approach, style, design or model that would make it doable. Could they relax their expectations or mental image of the future pool? Could the design be ished in regard to the size, or tile choice, or depth? Maybe an inflatable pool will do for now (that's very ish!)

Acceptable

Will ish be tolerated or accepted for this task, service, activity or project? Are there particular standards or criteria that need to be met? Would ish be allowed?

In some industries, communities, fields or societies there are certain norms, rules and regulations that mean you can or can't do certain things. You'll know if ish isn't acceptable in your workplace because you'll be following procedures and meeting standards. I immediately think of people in food handling positions, and pilots, and engineers and construction workers. An anaesthetist being ish during surgery is not acceptable at all.

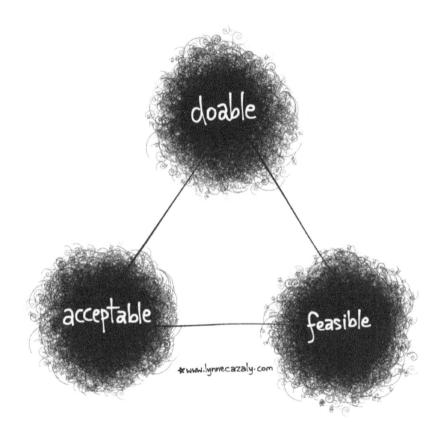

But what if the task has less impact: if it's less 'life or death'? Can we ease off our own high standards a bit?

We often impose our own invisible standards onto less important tasks. Think about your standards for washing the dishes at home. Does everyone in the household perform the task to the same standard? What about at work? Is there a different expectation? Maybe it's acceptable for you to leave your dishes in the sink for a while at home, but at work this relaxed attitude is not acceptable.

Is the workplace project gallery example acceptable to be done in an ish way? They will need to discuss the purpose and audience of the gallery and decide how professional it needs to look. The budget and time constraints for the project will designate where the line is between professional framing and hanging, and blue-tac and printer paper.

Pilots in aircraft follow checklists for this very reason. There are certain standards and regulations from regulators, governments and the airlines themselves (not to mention the actual physics that make a plane fly) that need to be met. When the standards aren't followed, there's an investigation. Because it wasn't 'acceptable'.

We have plenty of mostly invisible standards and expectations that we can't see and don't share with others and I believe we can let some of these lapse or at least we can ease off on them a little.

Many a customer service experience #fail is just this. The customer had an expectation, the company didn't meet it and it's a social media shitstorm of #fail to let you know just how it didn't meet their expectations. You'll hear and see people - even yourself - saying 'it's just not acceptable'.

The National Broadband Network is being rolled out in

Australia - about 15 years too late, but there you go, it's happening - and many people are suffering lower speeds than their previous ADSL connections. You'll hear, 'It's just not acceptable' from businesses in rural areas suffering from insufficient connectivity to do business, make transactions or carry out their day-to-day business as usual. So frustrating and just unacceptable, particularly when they've travelled to other cities or countries and experienced lightning speeds. Many a rural dweller has driven to the top of a hill in their area or driven closer to the next town just to get some phone service, 3G, 4G, 5G… whatever they can get is 'good enough' but in their eyes it could be better.

Feasible

Given finances, situations and circumstances, timing and other conditions, does it make sense to do this in an ish kind of way?

I'd love to travel to Iceland and go on an incredible 4WD trip through the volcanic regions, but it's going to be in the vicinity of $28,000 for a two-week holiday. This isn't feasible for me because of financial constraints right now. Can it be ished? Could I go for less time, or on a cheaper tour, or do a similar trip in a closer location? Would any of those be good enough for now? I could, but no. I have the vision of this trip and I'm going to hold out, because those ish options aren't what I want to do.

On the other hand, a workplace wanted to get iPads for each of its 28 team members, but there just wasn't the budget for it. Could this idea be ished? Could they get a different (cheaper) brand of tablet? Or share an iPad between several people? Yes – this was much more feasible.

In assessing for ish, if you still think ish is not a goer for you or your project - that is, ish is not doable or acceptable or feasible, then what might you really be rejecting? If the criteria don't apply or you think your activity, task or project is special and can't be ish in any way, then what are your criteria for that?

I've worked with numerous people providing mentoring and coaching services and often I'll hear the response of 'that doesn't work for me' or 'this doesn't apply to me' or 'that's not how I work' or 'that doesn't do it for me'. All of these are negations against invisible criteria and dare I say … an excuse.

What if they tried? What if they had a go?

They're saying 'it's just not acceptable to me' but I think there's an opportunity for some ishness there. And they will be the richer for it. In this way, ishing things could be one of the most effective strategies of 'getting out of your own way'.

The potential to ish

Here's the table I use to tick off the potential and possibility for ish. At work, it helps identify different standards and opens up that conversation.

You can put the tasks or projects down the left-hand side and then ticks or comments regarding whether ish is doable for this thing, whether it would be acceptable, would it be allowed, and then is it feasible.

To ish or not to ish	Is ish doable	Is ish acceptable	Is ish feasible
Project, Task or Activity 1			
Project, Task or Activity 2			
Project, Task or Activity 3			

I like to ensure people have a conversation about what and where they can ish at work, asking questions like:

- Will it matter in the short term, medium term, or long term?

- What are the short-term, medium-term or long-term impacts?

- Do other people need to approve the ishness of this?

- Who will be impacted?

- What might the cost be?

- Can different parts of this project or task or activity be ish? That is, if not all, then which part/s?

Just like the popular criteria for the 'triple bottom line' addresses 'people, profit and planet' (and, more recently, the quadruple bottom line now adding 'purpose') these are criteria that can be used in business to help make decisions and guide activity for ish. It's all designed to stop wasting time and energy pursuing perfection, a place that we know doesn't exist.

When not to ish

Ish is great, you can tell I'm an advocate, fan and all-round ambassador, except … there are some situations when ish isn't good enough.

Ish in times and places when the highest quality is required is just plain stupid and dangerous.

All over the world, in all sorts of industries, there are standards to be met. Ish is not about compromising these. When you stuff up things that should have met a certain standard, that's just slack and lazy work. Adopting a 'good enough' blasé attitude here is asking for trouble when specific standards are required.

Ish isn't good enough in situations like these:

- Poor quality, non-existent or ignored building codes particularly in areas where extreme weather occurs such as cyclones, earthquakes and superstorms.

- Craftsmanship, workmanship and attention to detail on tools or devices that matter. Think of surgery, construction, electrical appliances and other mechanical things that can result in horrific injuries and death.

- Civil and structural engineering like bridges, roads and buildings and pipeline systems.

- Constructions and facilities like oil rigs, hydro schemes, nuclear power stations.

- Do-it-yourself renovations and practices where people are at risk of injury, or worse.

- Aviation, avionics, defence and space travel.

- Other modes of transportation and their support systems like railways, trams and buses, motor vehicles, bikes, boats, scooters and drones.

I'm sure you can think of many others.

A whiff of danger

In my early career in consulting and communications, I was a sessional lecturer in public relations and communications at several of Melbourne's universities. Each semester the students in the subjects would research an assignment and deliver a presentation on crisis public relations. This is where a company, brand or individual has had a shocker of an experience: a natural disaster, a mechanical failure, an outbreak or loss of control over a system or a lack of judgement and governance.

Every single crisis presented on was at some time only a whiff of danger. That is, there was always a warning sign, or series of issues that were left unattended or ignored, or a system or process had limitations and was never updated or changed. It was inevitable in many of the cases that a crisis would hit; it was just a matter of when.

Students presented on theme park accidents, building collapses, product tampering, oil spills, disease outbreaks, landslides, floods, mine disasters and mechanical failures in the air and at sea.

The warning signs (that were ignored before the disasters) were indicators that ish was happening where it shouldn't have been. Customer complaints, feedback from focus groups, anecdotes and stories from staff on the front line are all whiffs of danger that something is amiss.

It's why Issues Management is one of the best things an organisation can do to monitor 'what's going on' and 'what's our reaction and response to that'. Best of all, this subset of public relations recommends businesses prioritize the issues on an issues log so that those deemed to have the greatest impact and consequences are dealt with – and quick.

In public relations, we would always think that any unattended audience or issue is just asking for a crisis. And no one wants a crisis. It's the result of inaction, the wrong action and the wrong type of focus.

It's a shocking reminder to keep ish for the things that don't matter so much, and in the important situations in work and life, to aspire for quality, excellence, iteration and improvement (note how I didn't say 'perfection').

An example of ish gone wrong

A current and ongoing crisis is the Takata airbag recall. Thousands, perhaps millions, of motor vehicles the world over are impacted by a faulty product created by a safety company. It's turned out to be the largest automotive safety recall in history.

If you've read anything about it or checked your own vehicle's status, you'll find that the problem is a faulty airbag inflator that has been linked to deaths and injuries. At April 2019 the death toll sits at twenty-four.

How did it begin? What happened? Did the company ish when they shouldn't have? Yes – Takata identified some cost-cutting strategies in the manufacturing process, and used ammonium nitrate as an airbag inflator that works at the time of impact in a car crash. But experts reckon this compound is sensitive to temperature changes and moisture, breaking down over time and then … combusting, violently. It's a cheap compound and it doesn't belong in a safety item like this. It belongs in industries that use it for demolition like mining and construction.

This is an example of ish where it shouldn't be.

Yet Takata found a market for the cheaper compound – General Motors. The original supplier of their airbags, Autoliv, just couldn't match the price and didn't want to use the compound so they ended their contract with GM. When incidents occurred, the recalling of vehicles began and manufacturers ended their partnerships with

Takata.

In 2017, the US government indicted three Takata executives and fined them $1 billion for concealing and tampering behaviours. Similar charges have been laid with executives in Japan.

Takata has filed for bankruptcy.

Many people in many roles and situations during the design, manufacturing and testing of these Takata airbags signed off on ish.

It was never good enough.

ish

CHAPTER 6

The how to ish bit

'Entire markets have been transformed by products that trade power or fidelity for low price, flexibility, and convenience.'

Erin Biba

Ish is about following a path to progress rather than pursuing the unreachable state of perfection.

And it's a choice you can make. Perfection doesn't exist, but progress does.

From default to direct thinking

In order to start acting and thinking more ish, we need to interrupt some of our default and automatic behaviours. It's so easy to just follow our ingrained habits – whether that's what we eat for breakfast, when we go to the gym or how many wines we have at the end of the day. Pursuing perfection is a way of thinking and it's an ingrained habit, likely formed many, many years ago.

I heard a neuroscientist colleague speak about our 'default mode network' over dinner one night. She said that a heap of our thinking patterns just slot right into a pattern that is our standard or default way of thinking. For example, if you're a bright-eyed optimist, this positive way of thinking is probably part of your default mode network. If you're into perfectionism, it's likely part of that default mode network.

It's kind of a relief, isn't it, to know that perfectionism isn't an incurable disease but rather a habit, or a pattern.

About half of the day we're in this default mode, responding easily and automatically in ways we've done before.

But don't worry; you can change what you want to change. There's another way of the brain working called the 'direct mode network'. Direct is about you being in control, directing your thinking. Now this sounds more like it.

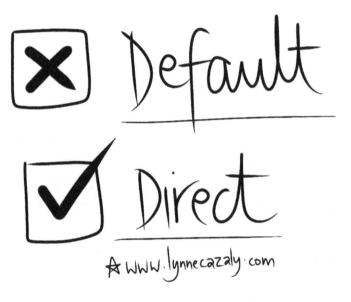

☆ www.lynnecazaly.com

To activate the direct mode network, identify the moment when your thoughts or actions start veering towards perfectionism. Pause your automatic responses and tell yourself 'Hang on, just wait a minute!'

Rather than thinking something isn't good enough or needs to be better (your default thinking mode), why not challenge that automatic go-to place and instead *choose* 'good enough'.

I was having lunch with a friend the other day and she was talking about some of the things she's working on: a couple of reports, a presentation, a client solution. Several of these projects weren't 'good enough' yet, she claimed. In her mind they weren't finished. There's her default mode right there: her thought patterns default to 'not good enough'. I challenged her and got her to direct her thinking, to consider that some of her work is indeed good enough for now. Way good enough. She could then focus – or refocus - on the stuff that actually, truly, really needed to be improved and worked on some more.

If we're putting attention on some stuff that doesn't really truly matter so much, perhaps we're missing some of the things that are worthy of more of our attention. We can switch on the direct mode network and get clear about it rather than being swept away on the wave of an automatic, ingrained, likely life-long habit.

So … ask yourself: Am I being a perfectionist about this? Is a ridiculously high standard really needed on this task or activity?

Oh, and you could always ask someone you know, a friend, partner, family member … they'll probably have some thoughts or observations about the standards you usually go for.

The foundation of ish

When I mentor, train or speak about ish, I explain two key things:

- Knowing when to start.
- Knowing when to stop.

The rest in between is great too, but we'll get into that later. Remember down in the depths, when things seem 'not good enough', down at the bottom of that ladder? Here it is again...

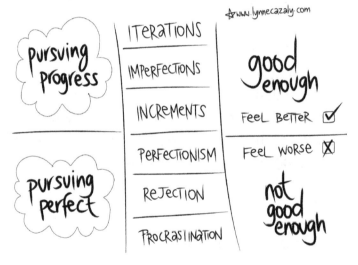

This is where procrastination and perfectionism hang about together. They're like bad buddies, influencing each other in ways that are unhelpful. We need to do something to split them up or manage them so they stop causing havoc and making us doubt and reject ourselves and the way good enough stuff we're already doing.

When to start – to beat procrastination

#www.lynnecazaly.com

Recently a client said to me, 'I can't launch my website until I've had my new photoshoot and I can't have the photoshoot until I've had my hair done and I can't have my hair done until my hairdresser comes back from overseas and she's not back for another six weeks.'

So the website has to wait *at least* another six weeks. Really?

There's often a condition we place on the sequence of 'I have to x before I can do y.' But is it always true?

Remember my story about the DIY business card? I didn't have a logo or branding yet, but if I'd waited to get that together it could have been months before I put myself out there. I'd just finished working a corporate job where my salary was automatically deposited into my bank account. Financially, this having my own business thing was going to be different; I'd have to generate the cash flow myself and part of that is putting yourself out there, not just hope that 'if I build it, they will come'. Now don't get me wrong, I'm as gifted in the procrastination department as the next person, but, luckily for me, at that moment my desire to put myself out there was stronger than my perfectionism. I see this with people putting their ideas or their business out there, busily working on things but not releasing, publishing, printing or sharing them. What's the true cost of this hesitation, procrastination, rejection and perfectionism?

I was mentoring a client, Tegan, guiding her through unpacking her ideas, her intellectual property and expertise so she could grow her consulting business. We got to the point when it was website time: she had some things to do and some decisions to make to get her web page started.

When she came to the next coaching session, she admitted that she hadn't done any of the things in readiness to build her website. It had been weeks, and she'd not made a start. To break her procrastination paralysis I grabbed my laptop, created a new trial account for her using free web software and started asking her questions.

'Which template? Choose one.'

'What do you want to call yourself? Decide on something – it's good enough for now.'

'What are the main topics of your services? Choose five.'

Despite me being there, holding her hand and guiding her through, it was a very emotional experience for her. Her months (actually, years) of oscillation, indecision and hesitation about a website were about to be dismantled. It was scary.

And what had been fuelling that procrastination? You guessed it. Perfection. She hadn't worked out the perfect wording or didn't have the perfect images or hadn't decided which would be the best website host or the right email address or the best description or the correct tone and style or the right type of branding.

When we made this rough but essential start, she was a bit shocked. She'd always thought it would be so much harder and take way longer. You know, writing a brief, engaging a designer, getting photos taken, engaging a copywriter … and yes, sure, you can do your website like that, later on. But right now, that wasn't the task.

'Come on,' I said. 'Let's ish it. Let's just get this first one done, then you can tweak it over time.'

None of it was perfect, but it was a start.

Making a start can be terrifying.

But is it better than not making a start?

We can hesitate and wonder and question and doubt and consider thirty-seven different possibilities ... but all of this is procrastination. We need to start.

And just as Tegan did, she *imagined* it was going to be bigger, badder, harder, longer and more challenging than it was in reality.

Here's our creative – and obsessive - mind at work, conjuring up a bunch of unreal expectations, situations, complications and scenarios that, most often, don't turn out anywhere near as bad or as difficult as we think they will be

★www.lynnecazaly.com

Our creative, conjuring mind is much better used when it is applied to the work, tasks, activities and ideas we have; not the things that we're worrying about or fearing. (Note to self, Lynne!)

Which option is going to help your new business: a beautiful, perfectly worded and designed website that exists only in your mind, or a basic, imperfect website that your potential clients can find? (As a bonus, having it up and out there will give you valuable feedback about what's working and what's not, which in turn will give you the motivation to improve it as your time, energy and finance allows.)

Ish is about not being immobilised by the fear of imperfection.

Ish is about putting it out there and seeing what happens.

It's about getting something started.

Think of those software developers: if they had waited until everything was 'perfect', they might never have made a start and we'd still be using typewriters and snail mail, physically walking into bank branches and calling travel agents to book a flight or hotel.

Set yourself a start point, a deadline, to get out of inertia and into action. There's a reason why Australian health and fitness expert Michelle Bridges has a countdown to the start of her online 12-week program; it's so people know when it starts, they have a 'go' point.

Without a 'go' point, you'll be hanging around with that baddie called procrastination. Not good company. Meh to that!

When to stop – to beat perfectionism

So we've established that perfection is an unobtainable goal (are you with me on this by now? I hope so). But at what point do we put something out there; how do we know when it's ready to share, ship or show?

☆ www.lynnecazaly.com

Have you ever created a PowerPoint presentation or a report? How many hours, days, weeks (and sometimes months) did you spend tweaking and tinkering? The thing will never be 'finished'. You can always, always, always add more.

Why are you doing it, do you think? The tinkering, the tweaking, the moving of the textbox a little to the left, the changing of the font and changing it again, making the font a little smaller or larger? Is it to fit better in the space that's available or to make it look good or to work better? What's the standard you're going for? Because at this rate, you'll be there forever!

At some point you will call ish on it. Maybe your eyeballs

are burning from too much screen time, or your kids need collecting, or you hit your deadline, or the night shift team arrive to clean the building. Hint, hint!

I was in a shop near closing time yesterday and a team member alerted me, saying, 'We close in three minutes.'

Quick! I got what I needed, good enough, paid and got out the door.

These external factors make you stop and allow you to let go of your quest for perfection: they let you ish.

So how could you call ish earlier? And to call it before you've wasted those precious hours of fiddling around and not changing much?

The answer is to set the goal posts before you start, and don't keep moving them (and don't let other people keep moving them).

Software development teams often talk about the **'definition of done'**. How do they know when a particular task or piece of work on a software app or software system is done? They define it. Then there's an agreement that, yes, that thing is actually done.

This is before they even start. How amazingly good is this as an idea? If you define 'done' before you start, you'll know when you get there. Plus, you'll see the destination up ahead and you'll likely be spurred on to finish the thing, lurching across the finish line, knowing where the end point is … the definition of done, the definition of enough. Good enough.

Let's say your hypothetical PowerPoint presentation is to sum up some key strategies for a team meeting. What does it need to be 'done'? Pretty pictures? Fancy animations? Inspiring quotes from awesome leaders in your field? Probably not. Your definition of done might be a few simple ideas per slide to summarise your thinking or supply supporting information. Deciding this up front will help you keep focused on what is needed, not on what you think it could be if only you had a few more hours, weeks or months. Once you have reached that point, your presentation is practical and fit for purpose.

You won't win any gold stars for staying back late to make it pretty or funny, (but you will win your colleagues' appreciation for making it succinct). You know when to stop. It is done.

The definition of done:

A key to ish is to set yourself some parameters before you get started so you don't lose yourself in a never-ending quest. Remember the software developers who have an agreed 'definition of done'? This is what you are doing here.

You are also making sure you know why you are doing it, what resources you have and what you want to get out of it.

Knowing this will help you decide where there's wriggle room to ish.

Before you embark on any activity, project, task or piece of work, take some time to answer these ten questions:

1. What do I need to achieve from this project?

2. Why is it important?

3. Who am I doing it for?

4. Is this the right time to be doing it?

5. What is my timeline?

6. How much time do I have to commit to this?

7. What happens if I miss my deadline?

8. What does it need to be fit for purpose?

9. What's the definition of done here?

10. What happens if I don't meet my goals?

Write these answers down and keep them handy. They form the brief for your project, which you can revisit and reset if you need to.

Download these questions and other helpful stuff at www.lynnecazaly.com.au/ishresources

To recap: when to **start** and when to **stop** are important foundations of ish.

If you're delaying starting something, call yourself on it. Bring your direct (not default) thinking to the party and ask yourself, 'Am I procrastinating here?' If the answer is 'Hell yeah!', probe a bit more and ask yourself, 'Why?' What are you fearing? Set yourself a starting point, like a deadline in your calendar, and just get it started.

Alternatively, if you're spending too much time on something, that is, you're trying to make it better and better because you think it's 'not good enough' yet, ask yourself, 'Am I aiming for perfection here?' If the answer is 'Umm, yes I think so,' probe a bit more and ask yourself what you're trying to remedy or make happen by continuing to work on this, despite knowing it's a waste of time, effort and energy.

And most certainly ask yourself, 'Is it good enough to go? Would Lynne say to me it's good enough already?'

How to ish: the pathway to progress

I mentioned earlier that ish is like a path to progress – getting the important things done – rather than a path to perfection, which is exhausting and depressing because it's never-ending.

I'd like to show you how you can make ish work for you along this path to progress. Follow the flags!

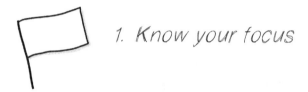

1. Know your focus

To help define your outcome or the point at which you'll stop, it helps to know what you're focusing on. Just like an astronomer peering through a telescope or a submariner peering up through the periscope or the surgeon peering along the endoscope – OK, too much information for some – you're homing in on your focus. The other stuff is blurry, out of focus, out of *your* focus, and irrelevant right now. Answer the ten questions in the box a few pages back to identify your focus: this is your definition of done.

2. Know when to start

To stop the paralysis of procrastination, you need to start. You can set a deadline or timeline, or have someone hold you accountable, or make a commitment to someone.

Alternatively, use a countdown timer or calendar reminder. I love a countdown timer either on my phone or online because it builds energy and focus as each day or hour passes. It is much more effective than saying 'I'll start on Wednesday' because that could mean 6 am or 9 am or 12.15 pm or 11 pm. I love seeing the countdown timers events – like conferences, marathons, summits – use online to build interest, energy and get people ready. There's no doubt that when the timer reaches zero, the buzzer buzzes or the alarm sounds that it really is time to 'go'.

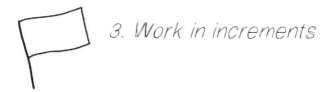

3. Work in increments

Rather than becoming overwhelmed by the w-h-o-l-e project or task, break the work down into packages, smaller packets or increments of work.

Who hasn't been overwhelmed by the sheer size and scope of an event, a report, an assignment – how do you PhD people do it? - or anything that involves lots of moving parts?

Have you noticed that companies like Amazon send out packages of books or products individually as they're ready? They don't hang on to all the items in your order, waiting, waiting, waiting until the final items are ready. They shoot the stuff they've got out the door. It frees up their warehousing, keeps the product and process moving and, in the end, is a more efficient way of working. There's less chance of confusion, greater likelihood of customers being happy with a partly fulfilled order, rather than waiting an eternity for all of it. This is an example of working in increments.

The totally glorious thing about increments is that you may only need to complete a few pieces or elements of this task or job and it will be enough. Seriously. And that's because ... drum roll please ... unless you actually work in increments, you won't know!

Starting with increments is how a lot of software developers batch up their work. They divide it into chunks or slice big projects and developments down into more manageable sizes. We need to do the same more often.

The software folks call their increments 'user stories'. These are the slices of work that will solve the problem for the user or customer who'll be using the technology or the app. They find that the thinner the slice (the more specific the increment or chunk of work), the easier it is to complete, and, of course, see when it's done. Boom! Progress. This makes us feel good; we're achieving stuff.

If you have to prepare a five-page presentation for work, rather than sitting down and writing the whole five pages from scratch, let's see what it might look like in increments.

- Work out the main point of the presentation.
- Outline what headings might be on each of the five pages.
- Source the necessary graphs, visuals and supporting information.
- Fill in the text under each heading, one section at a time.

The perfectionist might try to work on the whole thing, working across the breadth and depth of the whole project all at once, skipping from page to page, doubting the tone, style, design, content, colour, font, wording ... all at once. That's a sure path to overwhelm! Here's where and why it gets messy. It's because we're trying to tackle the whole thing, making it one BIG increment, one BIG chunk. It's too much for our mind, brain, heart to handle. Chunk it down into bites, slices or chunks.

Plus, who eats an apple in one bite? Ok a large animal. But humans? No, we slice, grate, dice, chop, puree, mulch, juice and pulse it. It's all about getting it into some increments we can work on, tick off … and that my friend is 'progress'.

And if you pick the most important or the most valuable or the most critical or the most vital stuff to work on first, then you're really working well, focusing on the increments, the bits that really truly count.

It's like planning a trip or holiday. You might book in your airfares first, get that sorted. Then lock down some accommodation. Then sprinkle in the side trips, entertainment, activities, tours. And then some other pieces to make some great memories and highlights.

We don't try and manage all of it, all of the trip all at once. Engaged peeps organizing their wedding try to do the same; not all at once, but bits of it. Invite list. Venue. Menu. Dress. Suits. Entertainment. Vows. Exchanging anything? All of these are tasks, chunks and things to do … increments and progress on the path to getting something done.

Be kinder to yourself by breaking it down. Who can cope with the enormity of it all? Not me! And I don't want you to either. This is one of the things sure to cause overwhelm. But chunks, steps and slices … this is working in increments. And it's freakin' magic I tell ya!

4. Know the required standard

You need to also define the quality – the standard – of the task or project.

Ask clarifying questions about what is required. Instead of accepting the brief, 'Write me a report by Friday', ask 'What do you need by then? Two pages? Twelve? Initial customer reactions or more detailed insights from all of the surveys?'

This is the key to stop pursuing the unknown, the unreachable and the undefinable perfection of someone else's invisible standards.

When you reach a defined standard, it is easy to know when to stop.

Like those athletes who know their focus, they also know the standard they're going for. They're aiming to finish in 1:12:46 (time), or a distance of three metres or a fastest lap time of 1:32 or an average lift of 98kg or to pass the Canadian world record holder.

These are all standards. Having them in our life, in our work, helps us reach them to a 'good enough' level – it helps us know and clarify what 'good enough' actually is - but it also helps us know when we can ish on our merry way towards them.

5. Let it be good enough

We are often not a good judge of the quality and progress of our own efforts. We're too critical. Remember the bottom half of the ladder, where we think things aren't good enough and it's the procrastination, rejection and perfectionism zone? Rather, we need to lift up to the top half of that ladder, and that means allowing some imperfection. We know now that there are benefits, value and reward in imperfection. We can let many more things be 'good enough'.

I was speaking with a colleague, Raj, who is preparing a learning and development program for a team. And I tell you what, he's just not letting it be 'good enough'. When we talked through the agenda and learning outcomes, what participants would be doing, how the program would run, what it would do for the participants … it sounded fantastic. Amazing. Brilliant and clever, creative and engaging.

But Raj reckons it's not good enough. Yet. He's been working on it for weeks. This is classic perfectionist behaviour. It points to the lack of a defined standard and focus – he doesn't know what he's going for or when to stop.

But you know what, it is good enough right now as it is. It is good enough for the first run of the program. It's good enough for Raj to go and get some feedback on it. Any more time spent on it and he's heading into the pit of great waste. Plus, the law of diminishing returns is right there waiting to diminish his future efforts.

'There is a difference between perfectionism and excellence. Excellence is knowing when good enough is good enough.'

Susan Peppercorn

 *6. Create prototypes*

To get feedback early and to check the validity or relevance of your idea or work, create a rough example that's good enough to show, share or get feedback on.

I'm certain we hold back because we're worried about criticism and rejection, and that something isn't good enough to show. It's not 'the best' we can do.

But this is the whole point of creating a prototype. A prototype is a pilot, a dry run, a sample, test or model, a mock up or an example. It's used to get some feedback on whether you're on the right track and whether there's value there and it's even worth pursuing any further.

Tech and startup industries use a development technique called 'minimum viable product' or MVP. This is a product (or project, idea, commitment) with just enough features to satisfy, and plenty of room to grow and improve following feedback.

I think you can MVP every damn thing! That means go with the absolute minimum effort or output that is viable and suitable for this situation.

This is part of the lean start-up movement. Lean processes began in the vehicle manufacturing industry where it was all about removing or reducing inefficient activities, wasteful actions and tasks that didn't contribute much – or enough – to the end product or outcome. And now new businesses and start-ups follow this principle to get a basic version of their idea out there, to see if it's 'got legs' and is valid.

Organisations all over the world follow this lean way of thinking, 'lean thinking'. It helps them streamline their processes so that people know what tasks they are working on, and they then zoom in on those tasks and do them to higher levels of quality.

They don't focus on extraneous activities that are time

and effort wasting.

They only focus on activities that deliver or contribute in a big way to the value or fidelity of the product or service for the customer. It's a less is more thing, which is so ish.

The minimum viable product makes great sense in other industries too. Any graphic designer knows that the mock up, the rough version, the rough layout is what's used to give a client an indication of what it will be like. They don't bother spending hours and hours and weeks on it; they do a mock up to say, 'This is kind of how it will look'. Architects do the same with those models of buildings, with little plastic trees and little cars and people. It's an early version to give people an idea about it. Imagine … just imagine if architects and builders had to finish the whole freakin' building before you could get an idea of what it would be like?

Even property developers of big fancy apartment projects have a 'display suite' that you go and check out to get a feel for what the finished project will be like. It's not the real thing; it's a mock up, a prototype and it helps them gauge interest and feedback from potential buyers.

I was looking at a building in Sydney the other day and they're still finishing off and fitting out the top floors, but there were people living and working in the lower floors. What the? Yes. They've built enough for it to be tested and tried out by real humans while they're finishing off the top levels.

The 'minimum effective dose' is a similar kind of concept used in pharmacy and medicine and the training and fitness industries and we can apply it to our productivity, our thinking, our efforts too. What could we do at the bare minimum and it still be good enough, it will still work for us, for it, for them?

When it comes to the prototype, it often doesn't even need to be a physical (or digital) object. Your mock up might be role-playing a situation or a verbal pitch or talking something over with someone or asking for some advice.

For each chunk, slice or increment, get it done as soon as possible and as well as you can. Go for low fidelity, MVP, good enough. Your goal is feedback at this point, not completion and most certainly not anything resembling perfection.

Prototypes help us counter what's known as the 'sunk cost fallacy' where we are so far down a path, we don't want to turn back because of all the effort we've put in. But sometimes it's plain foolish to keep going.

We humans sometimes find it difficult to give up on something we've put a lot of time and effort into. This can go for relationships, personal projects, investments, do-it-yourself projects.

Even if it's not the right course of action for us, all of that effort, time, sweat, drive and prioritizing one thing over other things, makes us mighty attached to it.

Perhaps we think 'it's not worth starting on something else' or 'I've come this far, I may as well keep going'. But no. It can absolutely be worth starting something else – and letting this thing be as it is, let it be ish – good enough - particularly if it has been gobbling up a tonne of time and effort.

If it doesn't work, or isn't viable, you can press 'stop'. Start again. Try something new.

Improvisers do it when a scene isn't flowing or going so well. One of the performers will wrap up the scene with something dramatic or a deliberate closing, or they'll shout 'Again!', raise their hands in the air, clear the stage and start with a fresh slate, a new prompt, clean air and a new scene.

7. Run some experiments (or know when to test)

Putting something out there before it's ready is a very ish way of learning if you are on the right track. It's going to help you get your product/book/website/service to where you want it, because you get valuable feedback from your customers/readers/clients.

To check on the validity of your ideas and progress, and to help you measure or evaluate, it's time to put your prototype 'out there'. The purpose is for testing and progress ... not for perfection. There's no need to fear the experiment; it's actually the thing that will give you insightful information that you can do something with.

This is the key to beating rejection and absolutely a key to beating perfectionism.

Scientists the world over run experiments all the time to find out if what they're thinking is the case. That's a hypothesis. They're testing, trialing, gathering information and finding out what's valid.

Every invention and innovation was once a hunch or hint of an idea. It was an initial draft or a first cut. It was most definitely ish; it was somewhat. No company puts something out there perfect on the first cut. There is iteration and improvement. Actually, there is accident too! Many discoveries and product solutions come through accidental ideas and imperfect collisions of thought. Unless you're in action putting things out there, nothing will happily collide.

Just look at Dyson vacuum cleaners. Now they're up to Version 11 and they've decided not to pursue vacuum cleaners with cords anymore. Did they know that when they started all those years ago? No. If they'd waited until they discovered that cordless was the way to go ... well, they would never have discovered it. It took years of people buying, using and feeding back to the company about how they wanted to suck up dirt, dust and dog hair.

How the heck could they work that out if they all sat there working at their desks, trying to be perfect in their engineering department, waiting until they created the perfect vacuum cleaner?

If you think they are pretty perfect now, it's because they've created thousands of prototypes and run thousands of experiments, tested, tried, evaluated, observed and measured what happened. Constantly. Continuously. They didn't make one and then they were done. Nor did they sit on the idea for months or years.

Now I see they've patented some designs and are researching a device for air filtering that looks kind of like a set of headphones. What an amazing application of their filter intellectual property. What a life saver that one will be. It's not ready yet; they're working on it of course, but you can bet they are testing heaps of different prototypes and versions of them.

Ikea tests its products and runs experiments relentlessly. I saw their 'drawer opening machine' – the thing that opens and closes a sliding draw on their kitchen kits thousands and thousands of times - doing its job in one of their stores. This is an experiment, a test. It's like a stress test on a new piece of equipment. It helps you find out 'are we on the right track?'; 'is this going to do the job?'; 'is it good enough?'

And hasn't chef Gordon Ramsay gone absolutely rogue – well he does often, doesn't he – to a contestant on a cooking show who hadn't taste-tested what they were cooking? He shouted at them, 'S-E-A-S-O-N-I-N-G!' Clearly the dish needed something more, salt, pepper, something else that would certainly have been revealed had the contestant run a taste test - an experiment - and got some insights and feedback from their palate or from a team mate.

With this information, a course correction is possible. The correction may be much smaller now than if we pursued hours and hours of work and ended up w-a-y off course, needing a huge course correction later.

It's a rotten feeling when you find out a lot of your hard work was not required. You can feel dejected, rejected and disappointed. You think about what else you could have done with that time that's now gone.

Without some experiments and tests on your ideas in their earlier stages, you're just asking for regret and disappointment.

Don't wait until it's 'perfect', test it out now. Test early and often. Find out how it works, how it's received. Be curious, wonder why ... discover.

www.lynnecazaly.com

Plenty of businesses are now seeing the benefits of having a kind of lab at their workplace; a space where it's allowed, where it's OK to run some experiments. And we can do that too! The famous Skunkworks initiative of Lockheed Martin in World War 2 has born many other imitators since, who set some people aside giving them the permission to go and be innovative, to test some things out. It's like a mini research and development project but we're doing it with an early, rough, incomplete version to test the water, see what happens.

For our project or ideas, an experiment could be:

- Like a taste test

- Asking someone to try something out

- Presenting something to people and asking them what they think

- Giving a sample to people to use and then watching what they do with it or talking with them about how they're using it.

I was on the beach in Adelaide, South Australia recently and saw a group of people rehearsing for a wedding on the weekend. All dressed in their casual clothes they were working out who was standing where, how long the vows would take, how long the music ran for. It was a big experiment. You could see them shuffling a few things around.

This is what we're doing. Test out your idea, talk it through with people, run it past them.

Some workplaces might call this a pilot. Whatever name

you give it, you're trying stuff out in the earlier stages of your work, rather than working those ridiculous hours trying to make something perfect – which we know doesn't exist.

Experiments save us time and bring us great information we can respond to.

The only way software developers improve and get better over time is by releasing code or putting their software and apps out there into the market, to their users and customers. From that release, users are able to provide feedback. Not just the 'Hey that's really good' type of feedback, but feedback in the form of information, data and insights, that together help the developers to understand what to do next.

It's not a judgement type of feedback; it's a helpful type of feedback.

I have a colleague who has started no fewer than four books. She had great hope each time. She's done great work to get them started, but hasn't been able to 'go live'. As soon as she is part way through one of the books, she changes her mind, changes direction and starts writing another book on another, slightly different topic. All that writing, all that work, all that time and effort and nothing 'out there' in the world to show for it.

I reckon she needs to test one of her book ideas … to test it out with a first draft, a first iteration. Yes, with an unfinished book. Let's look at the risks and benefits of sitting on an unfinished book versus going live.

	Sitting on it (Meh!)	Going live with it (Yeah!)
Risks	It's never finished. Don't get insights or feedback on your idea. So much wasted time on ideas that never see the light of day or are shown to others. Withholding and reducing your own success. Withholding valuable, helpful or entertaining information from prospective readers. Potentially not on the right track. Frustrates and impacts other people if they're waiting on	It's not 'finished' in your mind. It might be criticised. You might feel foolish or like an imposter. What if it doesn't work?

		your book and your ideas. You're all talk about these great ideas but nothing ever comes of them. You create an opportunity cost; what else are you missing out on by continuing to keep hold of it?	
Benefits	No-one knows you started yet never finished – the ego stays intact. More projects piling up might make you think you're creative and clever. Don't have to expose yourself or be vulnerable. Feel safe.	You are on your way. It motivates you to get onto the next draft. You get feedback to see what's working. You start to build a following. You're demonstrating you can get things done. Your work will get better via insights, input and feedback responses. It will become easier; you'll get used to working this way. The next book will be easier.

Leanpub is an example of a website where many people share their in-progress book-writing 'great work'. They don't keep it a secret until it's finished; this is about work that's in progress and the authors are able to receive feedback about it. They create, share and sell it there. So très ish!

So ish in fact, it's kind of what I've done with this book you're reading. I had early versions – experiments – available via my website and plenty of people bought these early versions and gave me their feedback on the work I'd done so far.

Then from running an experiment with your prototype, what happened? Get on the other side of the experiment so you can make sense of what happened.

- What might need to change?

- What options do you have now?

- What might the next version need that this didn't have?

A colleague is putting a new social media strategy in place for her business. Guess what? She's run some experiments and she's watching what's happening with responses from her followers and connections; which posts with which information seem to drive the greatest and deepest connections and which comments and ideas have the greatest impact in generating leads for her business. Boom! Experiment. A good boom!

8. Work in iterations

To lift the quality and strive for better (not 'perfect'), it's best to work in iterations.

Whatever feedback or results you received from your prototype and experiment, you can now put the insights to work, making adjustments, improvements and changes as you need to or choose to. You'll create a more advanced or higher fidelity version of your work to put out there and test again.

At each of these stages, the work we put out there is 'good enough' for the stage it is at, for the purpose of that stage.

It's good enough to run an experiment with.

It's good enough to get some feedback and insights on.

It's good enough to go.

This is great progress indeed. Working like this is so much more productive and rewarding – it makes us feel so much better - than sitting, waiting, procrastinating and chewing up time and energy pursuing pointless nowhere-land perfection.

Fancy pancakes for breakfast? There is a Russian idiom that says (in a modern spelling) **ПЕРВЫЙ БЛИН КОМОМ**, which means 'the first pancake is always a lumpy one'. When you've created the batter and whipped it up and you pour it into the pan, the pan isn't perhaps at optimum heat yet or the spatula isn't warmed up or the pan hasn't even had the pancake mixture on it yet. The first one isn't going to be the best one. Later ones will look much better. So we need to allow for some lumps in things. This applies to anything we're doing. Don't stop at version one, there is better to come. High quality doesn't come on the first attempt – we'll have to go again, and again. And again.

If you have a look at the version of any app you're using on your smartphone or the version of a software application on your computer you'll find that it isn't Version 1. Even new apps will have gone through a few versions, perhaps 1.456 or 2.32 or 10.3.4.56 or some other numbering system that lets the creators know what they're up to.

Looking at the Evernote app I use to collect a lot of my thinking, ideas and resources for book writing, it's up to Version 8.6.358974.

We're using products, technology and services every day that have been through so many iterations and changes. It's time to let go of those expectations of perfection on our first attempt … our first attempt at anything!

Rather than perfection, go for iteration. Remember, iteration means repetition … a new version of something.

It's been suggested that Amazon - fully loaded with apps and software brimming from every pore - releases updates every 11 seconds. Yep. Another update issued while you were reading this sentence. They are constantly and continually updating and iterating, improving and reissuing information and data on their website so that it's up-to-date and that features put out there earlier are iterated, improved and tweaked over time.

And it's great to see that the software peeps themselves have an 'International Remove a Feature Day'. It's in November and it sees teams working on software apps retiring features that have stopped being a vital or effective part of the app or program. As John Cutler, a 'product development nut' (he calls himself) with Amplitude HQ, said in a tweet: 'the collective usability of the world's products will improve. I'm excited.'

Here's this lean way of thinking, removing the unnecessary and the waste. Like!

Above all, we know this method works. The apps on your phone and the websites you interact with were pretty much all created by using increments, prototypes, experiments, insights and iterations (think of how often your apps get updated!)

Someone recently shared pictures of Uber's first website. Oh my, it's so basic. But it's what helped them progress towards the successful and popular app and service that works today. Same with Amazon; the first website, the first offer was pretty lame looking compared to today's finished version. So why are we expecting our own website or our product description or a presentation or report to be so perfect on our first attempt?

With iterative activities, you're aiming to get closer and closer to an ideal outcome. Over time. In software development, you're looking to lift performance or remove bugs or speed up or get better, quicker, clearer. Every cycle is called an iteration.

I believe we can generalize and apply this to many other tasks, industries and situations. You're getting closer to your target or goal with each cycle.

Rather than perfection, let's go for iteration.

 9. Know when to stop

Sometimes external factors will force you to stop working on something, for example if you hit your submission deadline or the date of a big event. Time has run out.

But other times, we can ish on purpose; we can call 'good enough' anytime, knowing we're putting an early or a rough version out there for the purposes of testing, trialling, learning and then iterating.

Most people I work with think that their 'stop' point on their task or project is further ahead than it actually can be. You can bring the due date, the end point, the 'go live' moment closer to you. Remember the 80/20 Principle. We've probably done enough and anything more we put into it could be wasteful.

Set yourself a fair amount of time and a defined end quality for the importance of the task, and stop when you reach it. Pushing it out or working until the last second reeks of perfectionism.

So there we have it, 9 steps on the path to progress where you actually get somewhere. You shift from the bottom of that ladder of procrastination, rejection and perfectionism, where we're thinking 'not good enough' and up into the cleaner, clearer air of 'good enough', the land of increments, imperfections and iterations. It makes us feel better, we make more and better progress and it allows us to ish on things where it's doable, acceptable and feasible, and save the quality, excellence and higher standards for the stuff that actually demands them.

Whether it's for the same project or for something new, get used to the feeling, the experience, the process of iterating and improving on the earlier versions of things.

It's more inspiring for us because it delivers us progress; we end up with a better result because we find the things that work or are needed – and we don't waste our time doing the stuff that's not necessary; plus … we're learning at the same time.

If we just kept working on it until we thought it was perfect, we'd hinder our learning experience and we'd end up wasting a tonne of time … and we create an inferior result.

Who wants any of that stuff? Nope.

'Only once you give yourself permission to stop trying to do it all, to stop saying yes to everyone, can you make your highest contribution towards the things that really matter.'

Greg McKeown

Sprint and then s-l-o-w

To help us ish, we can learn and apply an understanding of how rhythms work.

We listen to music, watch waves and are often hypnotized by the hum of an engine.

And while you're reading this, the best rhythm-maker of all – our heart – beats out a rhythm that can tell a cardiologist or other medico so much about what's going on in there.

It's worth checking out how being a little more rhythmic-ish could be helpful for us. We have circadian rhythms, the natural waking and sleeping times of each of our 24 hours. And there are longer infradian rhythms like a menstrual cycle's 20-something days. Other rhythms include blinking, our bowels and our appetite!

Of direct relevance to ish is ultradian rhythms. They're helpful when looking at sleeping patterns. I've found I'm less stressed when I focus on getting several good 90 – 120-minute cycles of sleep a night – and a week - rather than berating myself for not being asleep for a solid seven or eight hours.

Most fitness fans know the benefits of the workout and rest / recovery cycle. Professional athletes too. Their schedules include high and low-intensity segments along with rest, recovery and recuperation. They know it's the tapering, the recovery that is more important than the training - giving the body time to repair and rebuild, ready for the next onslaught. They'd certainly know about it if they didn't rest. Many a sports elite has returned to the field too soon after an injury only to do it again and then need a longer swag of time to properly recover this time.

The software development field has learned and applied this in their sprints of work over shorter periods of time from the 25-minute Pomodoro Technique to longer periods of time like two weeks. It sure beats slogging away at a project for months with no rest, return, reward or relief.

With ish, rather than going for constant levels of high peak perfection pursuing performance, let your foot off the gas. Go for shorter bursts of activity.

We're built for this.

Burst and recover.

Sprint and then slow down.

You'll be surprised at what you can achieve and how good you'll feel.

What to do when...

When you're stuck deep in the pit of pursuing perfection, it can be tricky to lift yourself up and out of it. Our minds go to doubting rather than progressing, and we can second guess and wonder, worry and whittle away precious time, effort and energy.

If you find yourself buried in the details of your project, and the end seems nowhere in sight, try this: these three little steps to get you out of the depths and into the clear air:

1. Stop ... and then scan

2. Revisit and reset

3. Proceed

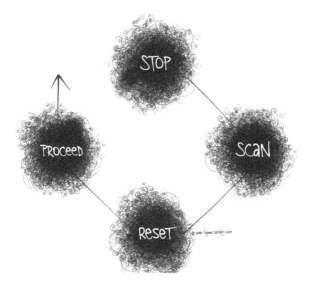

1. Stop ... and then scan

What are you actually working on? Make some mental or physical notes about this. What are you doing? What are your specific activities? Make a visual pass over your actions, not just your thinking. If you're too deep in thought and too shallow in action, you won't be getting much done.

Coming up to the surface for a scan is a handy opportunity to pause and get perspective. Submarines do it with the help of a periscope. We're just lifting our head up, having a look at what's going on.

2. Revisit and reset

Revisit your brief and reset your priorities if you need to.

You might need to reset the expectations of others you're working with or collaborating with or who are waiting on you. Don't be an island. Let others know what's happening, or why you're stuck. Things will become a lot clearer for everyone. Phew!

3. Proceed

It's time to get going again. The scan will have given you some perspective of where you're at, and you may have reset your priorities. You have a goal and a focus again. You may even have realised it's time to put it out there.

My client Sasha is a business analyst who works in the technology team of a bank. He was working on a proposal for a solution for the banking website. Even though Sasha had the key criteria for the solution, and the problem was defined, he was getting lost in the details of the project, trying to make the proposal 'perfect'.

He started working back late, coming in early, and not taking lunch breaks. He mentioned that sometimes he just stared at the screen, not changing anything, but thinking thinking thinking (he's an analyst after all – but he's overthinking, yes?) 'How do I make this better? I don't think it's good enough yet. This is not the sort of standard I should be achieving.'

Ish was absolutely needed here.

Continuing to try to make the proposal perfect was a waste of Sasha's time and energy. His time would be better used following the pathway to progress I've explained.

I said 'Stop and scan.' He stopped working on the proposal and scanned across the work he'd done.

Following the steps above, I advised him to 'Revisit and reset. Sasha revisited the outline for the proposal and the template used in previous examples. He reset his expectations against the work he'd already done and realised he'd already ticked all the boxes and had some great insight information from customers and potential users.

Next step: 'Proceed'.

Sasha decided to test out what he'd done. He shared the proposal as an ish version, using a watermark on the document. Sometimes we might use 'draft' or 'FYI – for your information' - in the background of every page of a document to let people know it's not done yet. I've been working with some teams and businesses where we've adopted an ish way of thinking and working and so using a watermark that says 'ish' let's the team know what the creator intended.

So Sasha used 'ish' as the watermark (part of the resources at www.lynnecazaly.com/ishresources) and he explained that this was an early version of the proposal and that he was seeking responses, comments and early feedback before he went any further on it.

I see this is different to 'draft'; sometimes a draft communicates that it's the first complete version, but with ish we might only be presenting the main, most important or most valuable chunks or slices.

So while that proposal was out there being commented on, Sasha was able to start working on some of his other tasks. When the feedback and comments came back, he made adjustments to the first version, tweaked it, iterated it and was able to send it through to the team who were in charge of allocating the money for the solution. Done. He was thrilled he'd made progress. Definitely up the ladder, in the fresh air, feeling better about it, making progress … not down in the grime of not good enough, feeling worse for wear. Good stuff!

How might they ish?

A lecturer colleague of mine was preparing for a new semester's program. They had a brand-new cohort of millennials in the course and they asked me how ish might be able to work for them as the lecturer. They explained to me their goal as lecturer was to make it 'the best course those students have ever attended'.

Oh, my! To prepare and achieve 'the best course they've ever attended' is a mighty big, undefined target.

If you don't know the students yet, how do you know what they want, like, expect and require? And what would make it 'the best' they've 'ever' attended? For all we know, the best course they've ever attended might mean sleeping all day, listening to music and finishing up with drinks at the local watering hole.

OK, yes, there are standards and learning outcomes and specific things the academic elements of a program require, sure. These things can be achieved.

But if we start designing the program with 'the best course they've ever done' as the target or goal, we may never get there! That's an awful lot of hoping and wondering and an incredible amount of work that might all be for nought.

Here's what I'd do if I was required to design a new course or program:

-   Create an outline of the subject and prepare the first

lecture. This is a smaller increment of work. I'd write one lecture. Not twelve. This will take a few hours' preparation, not weeks and weeks. This is now going to be a bit of an experiment.

- I'd then deliver that first lecture – a prototype of sorts – and have a conversation with the students to work out what they needed, how they liked to learn, and what engaged them. This way I'd gain input and insights, feedback and valuable information and would be able to put that into the next increment of work and iterate the program from there.

- I would choose not to see student – or any - feedback as judgement or criticism, but rather that I am co-designing the sessions with them. In this way I'd be meeting the specific outcomes of the program yet facilitating it in a way that's efficient for us, meets the students' needs *and* delivers something that is a win for us all.

Here's where increments of work, prototypes with that work, experiments of that work, insights about that work and iteration of that work is so very, very smart.

That's increments, prototypes, experiments, insights. And then go again. With another increment, another bundle of work. This is more likely to deliver something that is acceptable and valuable to the students; plus it's doable as the lecturer and feasible to the institution … and ish is most certainly possible.

CONCLUSION

The final bit

'The pursuit of perfection often
impedes improvement.'
George Will

Perfection is on the rise – too many of us already suffer from it and more are developing.

The statistics are scary; the projections from perfectionist researcher Thomas Curran PhD in his TED talk say that by 2050 one in 3 young people will have clinically relevant levels of socially prescribed perfectionism. We know that the pursuit of perfection causes discomfort, disappointment, anxiety, depression and a host of other ailments that are no doubt putting pressure on the healthcare systems of the world and causing people harm, as well as wasting countless productive hours of work in many industries.

It doesn't have to be like this.

We don't have to berate ourselves, spend endless hours pursuing perfection or allow our other priorities, interests and opportunities to go by the wayside.

We can choose to **direct** our thinking instead of defaulting to perfectionist habits.

We can focus on what our **outcome** is.

We can define our end state, our **definition of done.**

We can **know when to start**, by working in **increments**, batches and smaller chunks, instead of letting procrastination paralysis set in or trying to work on the whole thing at once.

When we're doing the work, we need to accept **imperfections** – they're good, human, beautiful and part of us ... and they can work to our advantage, remember.

We can put our ideas out there sooner and **test** them even when they're in a rough or early version – this is how we make the best use of the time we have and ensure we stay on track. It saves time and pain later.

We can ask the questions that help define the **standard** we're going for. 'Perfect' or 'better' aren't definable.

We can try more **experiments** – adopting or having an experimental mindset helps us stay open, curious, learning and developing. This helps us continue to grow so we can cope with and make the most of the life we're creating for ourselves.

And we can use the wonderful power of **iteration** to improve on things over time.

Most of all we can **know when to stop**. Whenever we start burning the midnight oil, get stuck tinkering, or thinking it's 'not good enough, yet', let that be a warning sign that you're possibly, potentially, pursuing a path of perfection.

To feel better, enjoy life more and challenge the unrealistic expectations we have of ourselves, the expectations we think society has for us and the expectations we hold for others, we must be more willing to accept, invite and welcome imperfection. Not just tolerate or excuse it, but allow imperfection; let it be. Welcome.

'It's not that we have too short a
time to live, but that we
squander a great deal of it.'

Lucius Annaeus Seneca,
Philosopher

Life-changing benefits

I've experienced so many life-changing benefits from being more ish, more often … and I'd love for you to enjoy and experience these benefits too.

There's **more time available** to you, where you get to tick off the things on your bucket list, the things you truly want to do, the things that matter more. We become more in control of our life and more in control of the things we work on, create and produce. In this way, we're better at self-leadership.

When we're working with others, we're more flexible, **easier to get along with**. And this extends to our home and family life as well.

There's absolutely the benefit of **less stress** to be enjoyed. We become **less worried** about how things look, whether they're the 'right' quality, or whether they reach some artificial standard we've concocted in our creative mind.

Projects, tasks, activities end up getting done, sooner. And then we feel less busy, **less overwhelmed** with things to do. With more progress being made, we have that 'feel good feeling' when stuff gets done rather than berating ourselves for the stuff that's undone.

Ish helps us **identify what's important** to us – if we're not sure, working out what you can ish is a wonderful way to help us do that. You realise the things that do deserve your extra time, effort, love.

We know from the research quoted that perfectionism makes us feel less good about ourselves. So, less of a focus on perfect brings about **better feelings about ourselves.**

We get to **learn and experience more**, from things we might have previously tried to avoid. In that way we progress more in our skills, knowledge and development.

The feelings of success are more frequent when we finish the things we deem important, putting our ideas and projects out there into the world.

And did I mention time … there's more time to care about what we really want to care about!

The limited resource of time

There's the saying 'time is money' but most of us often don't act like that. We spend plenty of time on things that others ask of us – or expect of us or we imagine (perhaps wrongly) they expect of us – and every time we give over some of our time, we must remember to be just as conservative as if it were our hard-earned money.

Time is indeed the limited resource in life and knowing its value is an enlightening and life-changing place to get to.

There will always be plenty of things we *could* do. Which

of those things truly deserve our time, effort, energy and attention? Which of those things *will* we do?

Our clock of life includes time that we spend, time we lose and time that's stolen from us. Protect it and prioritise it.

ish

The
final
final bit

'It's impossible to be awesome at everything all the time so it's critical to identify the key moments that matter most.'

Ilya Prokopoff

If I was to explain the idea of ish – good enough – in the simplest way, it's...

... that we need to care less about more. We're too concerned about trying to do better on too many things. Our efforts get diluted, we get stretched in all directions and our minds get overwhelmed. Let's care less about more, hey?

And equally, why don't we care more, about less? Let's focus on the people, vital tasks and experiences that truly deserve our time and matter to us.

For parents reading this, help your children identify, celebrate and love their imperfections. Reward work efforts and attitudes over striving for perfection. We know that perfectionism can develop in children as a coping mechanism, but it can truly debilitate work and creative pursuits in the future.

Be kinder to yourself, and others, and actively choose a path of progress over a path of endless disappointment.

If you're a leader, keep an eye out for people pursuing a path of perfection – it may be that they're not clear about the standard required. Help them. Clarify what's expected. This is responsible leadership in a world where too many of us suffer from mental illnesses that are exacerbated by the pointless pursuit of perfection and the problematic and toxic cultures in too many workplaces.

And pay it forward.

The pursuit of perfection is something many of us have battled with, so if you've read ish and can think of someone else who'd benefit, why not share the book onward – or buy them one – letting them know you love 'em just as they are: that their imperfections are awesome and their decision to ish more in their life is just fine by you.

And if you're on the receiving end of several copies of ish … hint, hint, there's a number of people looking out for you and your wonderfully successful future.

Ish is a practice.

Ish is a way of thinking, being, doing. Of course, there are some things you won't ish – it's not always suitable or appropriate. But there will be many, many things you can ish and all will be well.

As you ish on more things in life and notice, like I did, that the sky doesn't fall in, people don't even notice, and you have more time, more energy and way less stress – you will have time for the things that matter to you.

You'll find you can become the boss of your direct thinking, loving and leveraging your imperfections and calling out your default thinking that has formed habits over a long time.

You don't need perfect anymore – that's because your good enough ... is way good enough. ✅

'Perfectionism is a dangerous state of mind in an imperfect world. The best way is to forget doubts and set about the task in hand... If you are doing your best, you will not have time to worry about failure.'

Robert Hillyer

The Problem with our
Pursuit for Perfection

ish

and the
Life-Changing Practice
of Good Enough

LYNNE CAZALY

Blank=ish ☺

References

Chapter 1

McCulloch, Gretchen. 'Ish: How A Suffix Became A Word.' *Slate Magazine*, The Slate Group, 9 June 2014. www.slate.com/blogs/lexicon_valley/2014/06/09/ish_how_a_suffix_beca me_an_independent_word_even_though_it_s_not_in_all.html.

Chapter 2

Tabaka, Marla. '8 signs you're a perfectionist (and why it's toxic to your mental health)'. *Inc.com* October 31, 2017.

Curran, Thomas PhD and Hill, Andrew PhD. 'Perfectionism is increasing and that's not good news'. *Harvard Business Review*, January 26, 2018.

Curran, Thomas PhD. TED Talk. 'Our dangerous obsession with perfectionism'. *TEDMED* November 2018.

Flett, Gordon L., and Paul Louis. Hewitt, editors. 'Perfectionism: Theory, Research, and Treatment.' *American Psychological Association*, 2002.

Landrum, Sarah. 'How Being a Perfectionist Really Is Your Biggest Weakness.' *Ladders* | Business News & Career Advice, Ladders Inc., 13 June 2018, www.theladders.com/career-advice/how-being-a-perfectionist-really-is-your-biggest-weakness.

Plummer, Matt, and Jo Wilson. 'The Lie That Perfectionists Tell Themselves.' *Harvard Business Review*, Harvard Business Publishing, 4 May 2018, hbr.org/2018/05/the-lie-that-perfectionists-tell-themselves?utm_source=linkedin.

Avgoustaki, A. and Frankort, J. 'Implications of work effort and discretion for employee well-being and career-related outcomes: an integrative assessment.' *Industrial and Labor Relations Review*, 2018

Chapter 3

Caprino, Kathy. 'I've Been Coaching Successful People for Years, and the Same Trait Holds Nearly All of Them Back.' *Business Insider*, Insider Inc., 12 Sept. 2017. www.businessinsider.com/the-dangers-of-perfectionism-2017-9

Caprino, Kathy. 'Why Perfectionism Damages Your Life and 4 Ways to Overcome it'. *Medium.* July 29, 2017.

Schwartz, Barry. Transcript of 'The Paradox of Choice.' *TED: Ideas Worth Spreading*, TED Conferences LLC, 2005, www.ted.com/talks/barry_schwartz_on_the_paradox_of_choice/transcript.

Godin, Seth. 'Perfect vs Important.' *Seth's Blog*, 17 Jan. 2018, seths.blog/2018/01/perfect-vs-important/.

Chapter 4

García, Héctor, and Francesc Miralles. 'Ikigai: The Japanese Secret to a Long and Happy Life.' Thorndike Press, 2018.

Pfetten, Verena von. The Things We Miss: A Violin Virtuoso Plays A DC Metro Station.' *The Huffington Post*, Oath Inc, 17 November 2011, www.huffingtonpost.com/2009/01/15/the-things-we-miss-a-viol_n_158188.html.

Chapter 6

Agile Alliance. 'What Is a Minimum Viable Product (MVP)' 14 February. 2018, www.agilealliance.org/glossary/mvp/

Also by the Author

Conference Keynotes & Presentations

Public & In-House Workshops

Training, Facilitation & Mentoring

About Lynne Cazaly

Lynne Cazaly is an international keynote speaker, author and mentor. She's known for her humour, straight talk and highly practical skills and insights. She is the author of five other books:

- *Agile-ish: How to Create a Culture of Agility*
- *Leader as Facilitator: How to Engage, Inspire and Get Work Done*
- *Making Sense: A Handbook for the Future of Work*
- *Create Change: How to Apply Innovation in an Era of Uncertainty*
- *Visual Mojo: How to Capture Thinking, Convey Information and Collaborate Using Visuals.*

She helps individuals, teams and organisations adopt new ways of working. She works with executives, senior leaders and project teams on their major change and transformation projects.

Lynne will help you think better, make sense of information and handle the realities of information overload with a range of ingenious processes, tools and methods. She helps people distil their thinking, apply ideas and innovation and boost the engagement levels and collaboration effectiveness of teams. Plus, she coaches and mentors people 1:1 to help them bring greater focus, efficiency and success to their lives.

Lynne is an experienced board director and chair. She is a partner with Thought Leaders Global and a Mentor on the Faculty of Thought Leaders Business School.

Lynne lives in Melbourne, Australia, with her husband Michael and enjoys travelling to speak, train and connect with people. As a mad #avgeek, she loves all things aviation, air traffic control, runways and airports!

See more at www.lynnecazaly.com

✷ www. lynnecazaly.com

The Problem with our
Pursuit for Perfection

and the
Life-Changing Practice
of Good Enough

LYNNE CAZALY